The Pardoner's Tale

Geoffrey Chaucer

Guide written by
John Mahoney

Charles Letts & Co Ltd
London, Edinburgh & New York

First published 1988
by Charles Letts & Co Ltd
Diary House, Borough Road, London SE1 1DW

Illustration: Peter McClure

The authors and publishers are grateful to: Oxford University Press for their permission
to quote from David Wright's translation of the *Pardoner's Tale* from *The Canterbury Tales*
published in 1985 (p14); the British Library for their permission to use the lines
reproduced from the first edition copy of the *Pardoner's Tale* held by the British Library;
facsimile printed by Perdix Press in 1984 (p15).

This series of literature guides has been conceived and developed by John Mahoney and
Stewart Martin.

John Mahoney has taught English for twenty years. He has been head of English
department in three schools and has wide experience of preparing students at all levels
for most examination boards. He has worked both in the UK and North America
producing educational books and computer software on English language and literature.
He is married with three children and lives in Worcestershire.

Stewart Martin is an Honours graduate of Lancaster University, where he read English
and Sociology. He has worked both in the UK and abroad as a teacher, an educational
consultant and a writer. He is married with three children, and is currently Deputy
Headteacher at Ossett School in West Yorkshire.

British Library Cataloguing in Publication Data
Mahoney, John
    The Pardoner's Tale: Geoffrey Chaucer: guide. –
    (Guides to literature).
    1. Poetry in English. Chaucer, Geoffrey, 1340?–1400.
    Pardoner's tale. Study outlines
    I. Title   II. Chaucer, Geoffrey, *1340?–1400*
    III. Series 821'.1

ISBN 0 85097 844 0

Printed and bound in Great Britain by
Charles Letts (Scotland) Ltd

Contents

To the student

This study companion to your English literature text acts as a guide to the work being studied. Do not blindly read this book in the hope that it will replace your text: it *will not* and *cannot*! However, if you read it sensibly and sensitively you will see that it is continually directing you back into your text, the proper place for study. What we hope to do is to provide a vehicle to assist you to really **read** your text and gain greater understanding and insight into it, from which follows a real enjoyment of literature.

The major part of this guide is the Commentary where you will find a detailed commentary, analysis and questions for you to consider. It is hoped it will be a springboard to your own understanding of, and ideas about, your literature text.

Reading Chaucer

Do not work through your text, slavishly transferring the glossary from the back onto the narrative pages, or working from lists giving sound equivalences. The best way to appreciate and understand your text is to read it frequently and attune your eye to those very many words which will be familiar to you, despite slight changes in spelling.

The spoken sound of Chaucerian English is very different, and the best way to gain the feeling for the language is to listen to one of the many modern recordings that are available of the *Pardoner's Prologue* and *Tale*, read as it probably would have sounded in Chaucer's time. You might also try reading along with the recording; it is surprising how quickly you will gain a fluency in it, and also a better appreciation of the relationships between spoken and written word, meaning and intention of the author.

During the course of reading and listening to your text, many of those words which appear new or unfamiliar will gradually make sense to you. Check those which do not in your glossary, but do make this the last, not the first, resort.

Note on the editions referred to

Comments on the introduction to the Pardoner contained in the *General Prologue*, and the Host's introduction to the Pardoner (a linking piece between the *Physician's* and *Pardoner's Tales*), are referenced only to the second edition of *The Works of Geoffrey Chaucer* edited by F N Robinson and published by Oxford University Press.

In the sections discussing the *Pardoner's Prologue* and *Tale*, the first line reference is to F N Robinson's edition, as noted above, and the second to that edited by A C Spearing (*Selected Tales From Chaucer: The Pardoner's Prologue and Tale*, published by the Cambridge University Press). One of these two sets of line numberings will probably accord with your own text. However, there is also included a short quotation to assist you in placing a reference. If you refer to the 'Finding your way around the commentary' section on page 27, you will see clear examples.

The introduction to the Pardoner from the *General Prologue* is reprinted on pages 14–15. The manuscript version is from the Caxton First Edition, published between 1476 and 1478, a copy of which is held by the British Museum. On the facing page is a verse rendering by David Wright, from his translation of *The Canterbury Tales* published by the Oxford University Press in 1985. (Readers might be interested to know that he has also produced a prose translation, first published by Granada Books in 1965.) You will probably find it interesting and useful to refer to a modern verse or prose translation. However, it is suggested that, ideally, you leave such a reading until after you have gained a familiarity with the text as Chaucer wrote it. Equally, translations themselves differ in many respects, and if you are seeking clarification of the 'sense' of a particular passage, you would do well to look at more than one translation.

Geoffrey Chaucer

Born around the years 1343/4 and dying almost sixty years later in 1400, Chaucer lived at the time when the Middle Ages was drawing to a close, and when the Church was moving into one of the most turbulent phases in its history.

Chaucer was born in London, the son of a successful wine merchant, who was acquainted with court circles. Coming from a prosperous, well-connected family, Chaucer had all the chances he needed, and given his obvious intellectual ability and a society which allowed a great deal of social mobility, he made full use of those chances.

He attended school in London, where he would have acquired a knowledge of Latin and French. By 1357 we know that he had become a page in the household of the Countess of Ulster, wife of Edward III's third son.

In 1360 he was taken prisoner at Rheims during one of the campaigns of the Hundred Years' War. His close connection with royalty is further indicated by the fact that the King contributed to his ransom.

From around 1368 Chaucer spent the next ten years on diplomatic business, travelling throughout Europe. As previously indicated, he was one of a new phenomenon of the time, a socially mobile, literate layman, who was neither cleric nor lawyer. It was probably during this period that he would have met Eustache Deschamps, a French poet who was noted for his *Miroir de mariage*, a satire on women; the Italian, Boccaccio – famous for the *Decameron*; and Petrarch, a poet and scholar. Chaucer would almost certainly have read *La Divina Commedia* by Dante (who was also an Italian), which was an allegorical account of his journey through Hell, Purgatory and Paradise.

We know that in 1373 he visited Genoa and Florence and that he was in Milan in 1378. It is believed he may have visited Spain, and there is every reason to assume he would have gone to both Paris and Flanders during this ten-year period.

By 1374 he had the Controllership of customs and subsidies on wools, skins and hides in the Port of London, followed by a whole series of official appointments. 1389 saw him in charge of building and repair works in the King's palaces as Clerk of the King's Works, an important and responsible office.

Little enough is known of his private life. He married, around 1366, Philippa de Roet of Flanders. She was lady-in-waiting to Queen Philippa and later to John of Gaunt's second wife, Constance. It will therefore be seen that he married well and into influential circles. Records indicate that he had three children, two sons and a daughter.

Chaucer's wife died in 1387. In 1399 he moved to a house in the garden of Westminster Abbey. Chaucer died in October 1400.

His most notable writings span the period of 1369 to 1400.

1369/70	*The Book of the Duchess:* a dream vision of the grief of a lonely young knight.
1372/80	*The House of Fame:* another dream vision with the poet carried off by an eagle to learn about those in the service of Love.
1380/86	*Troilus and Criseyde:* a tragedy of two lovers separated by the Trojan Wars.
1387/1400	*The Canterbury Tales:* his unfinished masterpiece in which an assorted group of pilgrims each tell stories whilst on their pilgrimage to Canterbury.

Background to Chaucer's life and times

The world in which Chaucer lived had its boundaries largely restricted to what we would call Western Europe. The Middle East was obviously known, if only because of the great Crusades that had taken place between the 11th and 13th centuries ensuring a close degree of familiarity with its people. However the momentous discoveries of Columbus (1492), de Gama (1498), Magellan (1522), and Drake (1577) were still more than a century away. Not until the 16th century would we see the Reformation movement which split the Catholic Church asunder, though even in Chaucer's time there were ominous rumblings. (The pardoners' avarice and the sale of pardons were to be important catalysts in setting the Reformation in motion.) The major explorer that Chaucer may well have known about was Marco Polo (1254–1324) a Venetian merchant famous for his travels to, and his writings about, Asia.

For all the relative smallness of Chaucer's world, he lived through a time of great change and upheaval. 1327 saw the accession of Edward III to the throne, and in 1337 the Hundred Years' War began: a series of drawn-out conflicts between France and England, with the English attempting to reestablish their rule over large areas of France. The famous battles of that period, Crecy (1346), Poitiers (1356) and Agincourt (1415) have been long remembered in our history books, but other events at home were equally momentous and perhaps had greater and further-reaching consequences.

In 1348 the Black Death reached England and almost a third of the population perished within a year. It had far-reaching consequences. The population, not knowing what caused it and therefore lacking the ability to prevent it, could do little to help themselves. With many of the population dead, it was not very surprising that death took on an almost 'familiar' air. Contemporary art and literature reflect medieval man's concern with his visitations and it would not be too surprising if the people, en masse, took their religious beliefs and practices with a degree more seriousness! (The possibilities the pardoners presented to the people of their being able to purchase pardons for their sins and at the same time improve their material lot must have been very tempting.) The juxtaposition of pardoner with the pursuit and visitations of death in the *Pardoner's Prologue* and *Tale* should not, therefore, greatly surprise us.

One effect of the Plague was a lack of labourers in the fields which led to a sharp rise in inflation and disputes between the various classes in society. By 1351 the Government saw fit to introduce the 'Statute of Labourers' by which it sought to limit wages to the level before the Black Death and its ensuing inflation. With further visitations from the Plague in 1361/2 and 1368 matters did not improve; by 1400 the Plague had probably been responsible for halving the population. Shortly after the accession of Richard II to the throne in 1377, a poll tax was imposed, and as with most taxes it would seem, it fell very heavily on the poor.

In 1381 the Peasants' Revolt began, demanding the end of the poll tax and the abolition of villeinage–the tenure by which a villein held his land, bound to his lord and to whom he often had to pay crippling taxes. If you refer to pages 12–13 there is a facsimile of part of a map of Great Britain. Drawn in 1370, it gives us some idea of the medieval map-maker's conception of what the country looked like. More particularly, you will see marked on it the extent of the Peasants' Revolt, from Norwich down to Winchelsea, from Canterbury (our pilgrims' destination) to London and beyond.

The revolt brought widespread violence against clergy, tax collectors and landed gentry. Severe rioting took place in Canterbury, Maidstone, Rochester and Dartford, as well as in many other towns. In London a mob forced its way into the Tower and murdered the Archbishop of Canterbury and the Lord Treasurer. The poll tax was eventually abolished, and gradually the peasants gained greater freedom. It is against this background that we begin to see the depths to which the Pardoner plumbed in leeching on the poor people of the land, even to the extent of leaving the children of the poorest widow 'sterve for famyne' (1.451).

The influence of the Catholic Church was still enormous, and would continue to be so for many years. Even so, disputes of a political nature between Rome and London still occured. For example in 1366, Parliament refused to pay a feudal tribute to the Pope. However, with the putting down of the Peasants' Revolt, the nobles and landed gentry were concerned to reestablish their position and stability in the country, which inevitably involved stability in the Church. Accordingly, reformers such as Wycliffe fell from such favour as they had, and the Church retained its hold in the country for another two centuries, though along with the various political factions that abounded, it was usually an uneasy peace that reigned in the land.

A short literary perspective

With the Conquest, Norman-French was introduced to the country. During the course of the century after 1066, Old English was gradually replaced, primarily by Latin, which was used for business and learning; it was, of course, also the language of the Church. After Latin, French was the primary language of the educated and powerful.

English was relegated to the language of common speech, with a variety of dialects. It was largely unrecorded except for a very small body of written work.

During the course of the 12th to 14th centuries, Norman-French gradually became more of a social accomplishment, failing to gain any ground amongst the mass of the people. Latin continued to be a key language. Both of these languages were used for textbooks and documents, and their use and influence continued to be felt long after the 14th century.

The body of written work during the Middle Ages is not huge and of Chaucer's contemporaries only a few need to be considered here.

John Wycliffe is perhaps best remembered as the first Protestant. Born about 1324, he was a professor at Oxford University and became chaplain to Edward III. He attacked the concept of papal supremacy, and the hierarchy of the Church. Gaining little real support from the court he decided to appeal to the people of the country. It was at this stage, 1380, that he began to write in English instead of Latin. Most notably, he translated the New Testament into English, being responsible with others for the translation of the entire Bible. However, he turned gradually to attack the popular devotions to the saints, and more importantly the idea that the Eucharist was not actually Christ's body and blood, but only a symbol of it–an idea which undermined the whole basis of Christian beliefs of the time. It is worth considering whether some of his ideas on this subject are repeated in the blasphemies found in the *Pardoner's Tale* and *Prologue*. His friends eventually abandoned him and he died peacefully in 1384.

Composed sometime around 1360–1370 are four poems which were written in the Lancashire dialect: *Pearl, Purity, Patience* and *Sir Gawain and the Green Knight*. Nothing is known of the author except that, from the internal evidence of the poems, he was familiar with courtly life and society and also knew the country. A central aspect of the works is the concern to praise purity and chastity.

Piers Plowman was written by William Langland who came from the West Midlands. Langland was born in Shropshire around 1332, and lived for a while in the Malvern Hills. He died in about 1400. The poem appeared in three versions, each of a different length, in 1362, 1377, with the third and longest version appearing around 1395–1398. The poem concerns itself first with the evils that abound in a society which calls itself Christian, and then with a vision of what that society would be like if it truly followed the teachings of Christ. In this work, but in a more direct way, some of those concerns which seem to lie behind the *Pardoner's Tale* may be seen.

The other figure of note at the time of Chaucer was John Gower. His date of birth is not known, but he died in 1408. He was a poet, writing initially in Latin and French, but later in life turning to English. Called 'moral Gower' by Chaucer, he, too, was concerned with the morality of the age as well as other social aspects. Living as he did at the time of the Peasants' Revolt, and being one of the threatened class who so aroused their ire, his poem *Vox Clamantis* gives us another perspective on that event and its causes. His only work in English was the poem *Confessio Amantis*, a huge collection of stories; some of the poem's themes can be seen in Chaucer's work.

This is not the place for a detailed study of these works and their authors, and their relationship to the works of Chaucer. They are given merely to 'place' Chaucer in a literary context.

There were four major dialects which struggled to become the common language of England: Northern, Southern, and East and West Midlands. It was however the dialect of the southern East Midlands, a triangle bounded by London and the two university cities of Oxford and Cambridge that became preeminent and it is in this dialect that Chaucer wrote.

The Canterbury Tales

The framework for the *Pardoner's Prologue* and *Tale* is that of *The Canterbury Tales* as a whole. A number of pilgrims assemble at the Tabard Inn, Southwark, in preparation for setting out on a pilgrimage to Canterbury, to visit the shrine of Thomas à Becket. The host of the Tabard Inn, Harry Bailly, suggests that a story-telling contest should be undertaken to help pass the long journey there and back, and that each pilgrim should contribute a total of four tales. The plan for such a large number of tales was not to be fulfilled, and of the thirty pilgrims only twenty-three tell their tales, and then only one each. (Of course, the Host's description of how many tales there were to be may not have been Chaucer's final plan, but we shall never know whether he changed his mind, or just ran out of time!)

There is clear indication that the tales we do have were not previously prepared for publication by Chaucer. For example, The Second Nun refers to herself as an 'unworthy son of Eve'. Some tales were composed a while before the main body of the *Tales*, and had previously been referred to by Chaucer under different titles. The actual manuscripts were not arranged in any consistent order, so *Tales* told near to Canterbury appeared before some of those told just after leaving London.

As with many other tales, the *Pardoner's Tale* (that is the story of three rioters), had its origins almost in the mists of time. Its antecedents are traceable to the Far East, to a third century Buddhist text, but the source which Chaucer actually used is not known.

In the *General Prologue* twenty-one individuals are introduced one by one, in a similar vein to that of the Pardoner. (His introduction is to be found on page 29). The length of these portraits varies considerably, from but nine lines for the Cook to over forty lines for others, e.g., forty-five for the Prioress and forty-six for the Summoner and for the Pardoner. It is very probable that Chaucer modelled some of the pilgrims on people known to him, but whilst some interesting research has been done on this subject, no definitive exposition has been possible, not least because of the great time that has elapsed since first composition of the work. What is obvious is that the pilgrims are representative of a broad sweep of 14th century society, with the notable exceptions of royalty and upper ranks of the nobility. Individual pilgrims can be seen to exemplify various types of character and conduct, an obvious one being that of the Pardoner, a true hypocrite. Given the wide range of character types and professions, the tales they tell reflect an equally wide range of subject matters and styles. The tales also sometimes reflect the character of the teller and his vocation – again, as exemplified by the Pardoner.

Various pilgrims typify the range of social groupings to be found in their society. For example the military is represented by the Knight, his son the Squire, and the Yeoman who carried the Squire's arms. The professions are seen in the Doctor of Physic and the Man of Law. The peasants and artisans are represented by the Ploughman, Miller, Reeve and Franklin, and so on through crafts, victuallers, secular clergy and monastic orders.

The *Tales* are also comprehensive in the wide range of contemporary literary styles and narratives that they encompass: chivalrous romances, lives of saints, mock sermons (the *Pardoner's Prologue* and *Tale*), moral allegories, to name but a few. Some of the *Tales* also form natural groupings, for example, the *Wife of Bath's Tale*, and the following six tales are usually referred to as the 'marriage group' – so called because they all deal with an underlying central issue, the nature of authority in marriage.

As will be seen from the above, *The Canterbury Tales* form a complex and sometimes closely interrelated whole. Whilst each does stand on its own we do well to recognize and be aware of the context from which they spring.

Cantuaria

Mare Orientale

Yernemouth   Donwych   Orford
                                    Meres

Brumholm   Norwich   Yepeswych

Crowmere   Colchester
Blakeney   Tetford   Bery
                                    Chelmesfor
            Pykynham
                        Myldenhal
Walsyngham   Donemowe
                    Cauntebrege   Stortford
        Lenne
                        Elye   Wa
    Walpole   Huntyngton
    Spaldyng   Roysto
                                Ramsey
Boston   Croweland
Bolinbrok   Bedford
                        Petreburgh

                Sleford   Neghman
Horncastell
            Somertwn   Stamford   Northamp
Lincoln   Grantham
Stowe   Pakyngham   Davent
                            Okham
                Bevoir
            Newark   Leycestre

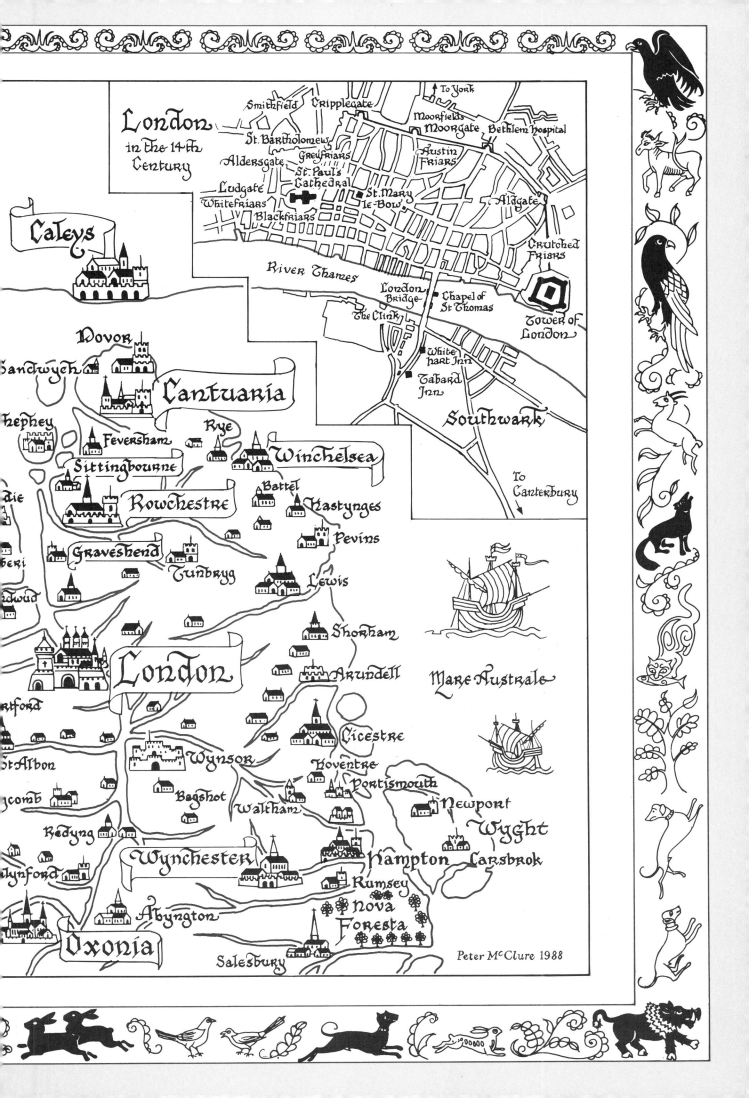

London in the 14th Century

Smithfield · Cripplegate · To York
St. Bartholomew · Moorfields · Moorgate · Bethlem hospital
Aldersgate · Greyfriars · Austin Friars
St. Paul's Cathedral
Ludgate · St. Mary le-Bow · Aldgate
Whitefriars
Blackfriars · Crutched Friars
River Thames · London Bridge · Chapel of St Thomas · Tower of London
The Clink
White hart Inn
Tabard Inn · Southwark
To Canterbury

Caleys

Dovor
Sandwych
Cantuaria
Shephey
Rye
Feversham · Winchelsea
Sittingbourne
Rowchestre · Battel · Hastynges
die
Graveshend · Pevins
Tunbryg · Lewis
Mare Australe
London · Shoram
Arundell
Hartford
Wynsor · Cicestre
St Albon · Coventre
comb · Bagshot · Portismouth
Waltham · Newport
Redyng · Wyght
lynford · Wynchester · Hampton · Carsbrok
Rumsey
Abyngton · Nova Foresta
Oxonia
Salesbury

Peter McClure 1988

With him there was a peerless pardon-seller
Of Charing Cross, his friend and his confrère,
Who'd come straight from the Vatican in Rome.
Loudly he sang, 'Come to me, love, come hither!'
The summoner sang the bass, a loud refrain;
No trumpet ever made one half the din.
This pardon-seller's hair was yellow as wax,
And sleekly hanging, like a hank of flax.
In meagre clusters hung what hair he had;
Over his shoulders a few strands were spread,
But they lay thin, in rat's tails, one by one.
As for a hood, for comfort he wore none,
For it was stowed away in his knapsack.
Save for a cap, he rode with head all bare,
Hair loose; he thought it was the *dernier cri*.
He had big bulging eyes, just like a hare.
He'd sewn a veronica on his cap.
His knapsack lay before him, on his lap,
Chockful of pardons, all come hot from Rome.
His voice was like a goat's, plaintive and thin.
He had no beard, nor was he like to have;
Smooth was his face, as if he had just shaved.
I took him for a gelding or a mare.
As for his trade, from Berwick down to Ware
You'd not find such another pardon-seller.
For in his bag he had a pillowcase
Which had been, so he said, Our Lady's veil;
He said he had a snippet of the sail
St Peter had, that time he walked upon
The sea, and Jesus Christ caught hold of him.
And he'd a brass cross, set with pebble-stones,
And a glass reliquary of pigs' bones.
But with these relics, when he came upon
Some poor up-country priest or backwoods parson,
In just one day he'd pick up far more money
Than any parish priest was like to see
In two whole months. With double-talk and tricks
He made the people and the priest his dupes.
But to speak truth and do the fellow justice,
In church he made a splendid ecclesiastic.
He'd read a lesson, or saint's history,
But best of all he sang the offertory:
For, knowing well that when that hymn was sung,
He'd have to preach and polish smooth his tongue
To raise – as only he knew how – the wind,
The louder and the merrier he would sing.

With hym ther wod) a gentil pardoner
Of rouncyuale his frend) & his comper
That streight was come fro the pope of Rome
Ful lowd) he song) com hidir love to me
This sompnour baar to hym a styf burdon
Was neuer trompe of half so greet a soun
This pardoner hadde heer as yelow as wex
And) smothe it hyng) as doth a strike of flex
By ounses hyng) his lockis that he hadde
And) ther with his sholdris ouer spradde
But thyn it lay be Culpous one and) one
An hood) for colde wered) he none
For it was trussed) vp on his walet
Hym thoughte he wod) vp on the newe get
Disshevelde saue his cappe he wod) albare
Suche glarynge yen hadde he as hath an hare
His walet beforn hym had) he in his lappe
A vernacle hadde he sowdid) vp on his cappe
Brette ful of pardon com fro Rome al hoot
A vois he hadde as smal as hath a goot
No berd) hadde he ne neuer sholde haue
As moche was it as it were newe shaue
I trowe he were a geldyng) or a mare
But of his craft from Berwik vnto Ware
Ne was ther nowher suche a pardoner
For in his male he hadde a pilow beer
Whiche that he sayde was our ladies keyll
He sayde he hadde a gobet of the seyll

That saint Petir hadde whan that he went
Vp on the se til Jesus crist hym sent
He hadde a cros of laton ful of stones
And) in a glas he hadde piggis bones
But with thise reliques whan that he fond)
A poure person dwellynge vp on lond)
Vp on a day he gat hym more mone
Than the person gat in monethis thre
And) thus hath he feyned) flaterie & Japis
He made the parson and) the pepill his apis
But trewli to telle at the last
He was in chirche an noble ecclesiast
Well coude he rede a lesson or a story
But alderbest he song) an offretory
For wel he wiste whan that song) was funge
He moste preche and) file a while his tunge
To wynne siluer as he wel can
Therfore he song) the merier than

Understanding the Pardoner's Prologue and Tale

An exploration of the major topics and themes

Do please note that the intention here is merely to explore, not to comprehensively and definitively chart. The latter task is not one that any critical work would sensibly attempt. Both this section and the Commentary endeavour to direct your attention to matters which you ought to explore further and dwell upon. The intention is always to direct you back into your text so that you really **read** it, hopefully with a mind open to the many possible interpretations which may be formulated from a work of literature. Careful reading and perceptive consideration of both this guide and the original text will enable you to adopt your own particular perspective of the work and derive from it a greater understanding and enjoyment. So read this text with the same open mind you should bring to the text you are studying, and feel free to disagree with what is written. However, do be clear in your own mind *why* you accept or reject any of the observations and always attempt to support your arguments with references to the text itself.

Summaries of themes

Audience

In a literary work it is not always central to an understanding and enjoyment of it to consider the audience for whom the writer was creating his work. One does need to be generally aware of the social, economic, political and literary background and the likely composition of the typical reading audience so that the literary work may be seen in its context. (The context in which a work was conceived and written is not of course the only one that is relevant: for example the political implications of Shakespeare's *Julius Caesar* have lessons for us today, just as George Orwell's *Animal Farm* is not simply a narrowly focused fable about the Russian revolution.) However, in the *Pardoner's Prologue* and *Tale* the audience plays an important part.

There is, of course, a universal aspect to the work in that the character of the Pardoner certainly finds its reflection in many a modern trickster, whether on the individual or corporate level. Undoubtedly he has his modern counterparts in religious terms as well, though the religious significance of his sins would not be so well recognized or accepted as central truths today, as they would have been in Chaucer's time. The modern audience, then, brings to the work a very different perspective from that of Chaucer's actual audience.

The audience to whom the Pardoner speaks falls into three categories: the 'lewed' people to whom he customarily preaches and from whom he gains the major contribution to his purse; the 'gentils or lordynges', his fellow pilgrims who provide the initial impetus for the story to be told and who may also become victims of the Pardoner's rhetoric; and, of course, the audience that Chaucer would have had in mind when he was composing the work and to whom it would be read. (If you bear in mind the crudity of the writing materials of the time and the lack of printing presses you will readily understand why relatively few would have the opportunity to read it for themselves.)

Because the Pardoner switches between the sermon, in which he demonstrates how he addresses the poor people, and the pilgrim audience, you need to be aware of what he is doing and, as importantly, what effect he is trying to have on his pilgrim audience. Different readings of the Pardoner's character may well reflect your estimation of the exact relations between the Pardoner and the other pilgrims and also your view of what intentions he had towards them. There is a vast amount of ground to be covered between a tale which is 'som myrthe or japes' on the one hand, and 'som moral thyng . . . som honest thyng' on the other, especially given the character of the story-teller. Could there indeed be differing readings of the Pardoner's character and intentions, or is he an 'open book'? Can some 'moral' and 'honest' thing be told by means of 'myrthe' and 'japes'? In considering the Pardoner and his tale you will need to explore his relationships with his audience in some detail if you are to reach any conclusions about the questions just posed.

Avarice

Radix malorum est cupiditas. The text on which the Pardoner preaches will be well known by you, but it is worth looking at the context of the New Testament from which it is taken. The full text will be found in 1 Timothy 6:10.

> 'The love of money is the root of all evils and there are some who, in pursuing it, have wandered away from the faith, and so given their souls any number of fatal wounds.'

It is also relevant to look a little further into what Timothy goes on to say, thus in 1 Timothy 6:17, he writes:

> 'Warn those who are rich in this world's goods that they are not to look down on other people; and not set their hopes on money, which is untrustworthy, but on God who, out of his riches, gives us all we need for our happiness.'

Consider some of the sins against which the Pardoner not only directly preaches but also mentions in passing: gluttony, drunkenness, gambling, blasphemy, lechery, evil intentions, flattery, hypocrisy, vainglory, hate, defamation of character. As indicated in the first quotation above, cupiditas is the one sin which under many guises gives the soul 'any number of fatal wounds'. It is worth noting the reference to 'fatal'. Has the Pardoner's avarice dealt a 'fatal' blow to his own soul, and is he instrumental in dealing such blows to other souls? Is his own sin against God the more serious because of the way in which he leads others into the same sin?

The Pardoner 'wol have monie, wolle, chese and whete'; would you agree his happiness is by definition a rejection of God who 'gives us all we need for our happiness'? From the gold the rioters expect 'In myrthe and jolitee our lyf to lyven'. Are the Pardoner's and the rioters' sins exactly the same? When you consider the many examples of sin which the *Prologue* and *Tale* give us, a little thought points the way fairly clearly to the scope of the Pardoner's sin of avarice.

The Pardoner teaches against avarice because of his own avaricious nature: the logic of this observation may not be immediately obvious. The Pardoner knows man's weakness and it is man's avarice in whatever form it may take that the Pardoner capitalizes on. Offering cures for jealousy (would this encourage both men and women into that same sin of lechery against which he will later preach?), increased crops and healthier cattle, all in the same breath as pardon for sins and glory in Heaven, he covers more or less all the conceivable needs of any man or woman. Because avarice rules his life, he uses the most effective weapon he possesses to achieve his aim – his knowledge of the character of man.

The Pardoner's message is a very compelling one, one that appeals directly to man's selfish view of self-preservation both in this world and the next, and ironically, not at all to his divine soul! His is a view that seeks to maximize personal comfort in this world, and minimize discomfort in the next. Whether or not you share the Christian values of Chaucer's world, or our own, would you agree that the Pardoner's message and methods offend against a much wider view of morality than just that of Christianity?

Background

Chaucer's world was very different from ours, in the quality of life and especially in the influence of religion on daily life.

Many of the allusions Chaucer makes would be understood by his contemporary audience, but we may not necessarily appreciate some of the nuances of meaning or the connections with current events or beliefs which the medieval mind would see. This particularly applies to matters of religious significance and concern for the salvation of one's immortal soul.

There is a whole range of topics about which Chaucer's audience would have been familiar: pardons and their abuse; other malpractices in the Church; the 'science' of physiognomy by which it was believed that one could tell another's character from physical appearance; the consequences of living in a rural economy; the pervasive influence of the Church and its temporal as well as its spiritual authority; the place which saints held in the hearts of men and the great devotion to them; the list is endless. However you do not have to be an expert on medieval history or the Church to appreciate the *Pardoner's Prologue* and *Tale*, but you must recognize that these matters make a very real difference to our understanding of Chaucer's work. The interested student will take some time out to read around the subject and sharpen his or her perceptions of what is happening in the narrative at every level.

Bible

The Pardoner makes many references to the Bible, and frequently calls upon it to support his narrative. Even today you possibly know people who take pleasure in showing off their knowledge of matters by quoting from various sources. In Chaucer's day, the number of sources was severely limited as compared with our times, but the most important source must have been the Bible. If the Pardoner was to support the image he presented to his audiences of being a man from whom it was safe to buy a pardon or relic, then the demonstration of being familiar with, and gaining, as it were, an endorsement from the Bible, was perhaps crucial to his technique. When you are reading the text, be aware of the uses to which he puts his knowledge; be aware also that no one was the wiser (or so he thinks) about the changes he makes sometimes to the Biblical references to suit his own purposes. Would you consider this another example of his rejection of God? The Bible is, after all, held to be the Word of God, and the Pardoner is but using it for his own avaricious ends.

Blasphemy

There are many instances of blasphemy (the use and abuse of God's name and power – a sin which would create a greater impact on the medieval audience than on today's) in the narrative, and they are important in creating the ambience for the story which Chaucer is telling. Given that many people of his time would have had the *Tale* read to them, you may imagine what use a competent story-teller would have made of them to illustrate and emphasize the sinful nature of the Pardoner and the rioters. Equally, the few blessings which come from the lips of the Old Man, and the strange blessing given by the Pardoner at the end of his *Tale*, must therefore stand in stark relief. What would you consider to be the effect of these contrasts on Chaucer's audience, both the pilgrims and those who listened to the whole narrative?

Boy

He has a small part to play in the *Tale*, but it is important in relation to his contrast with the rioters. The rioters are indicated as being 'yonge folk' yet in their wanton disregard for the realities of death, evidence for which is all around them, the boy provides a stark contrast. Note also how he helps to move the pace of the action along; there is no need for him to spend time finding out the identity of the dead man, he already knows. He is the first to introduce the knowledge that Death has recently visited this area, ominously killing 'an old felawe of youres' and then revealing that 'He hath a thousand slayn this pestilence'.

His appeal to the rioters to 'be war of swich an adversarie' is perhaps fated to fall on deaf ears, despite the evidence he had just given of how dangerous Death was. What does all this help to say about the rioters and the state of their souls?

You should also consider how the boy relates to the Old Man. Does the latter develop and amplify the warnings the boy gives, and also provide the means by which his warnings may come to fruition?

Church

The influence of the Church during the Middle Ages should not be underestimated. As both a temporal and spiritual power, it influenced every aspect of man's life, whether he was a poor villein or a king. It was manipulated by kings and nobles, and in its turn did more than just dabble in politics. There are many and well-documented examples of its malpractices, or perhaps more accurately those of its members, which contributed to a growing call for reform.

For all its ills the Church continued to produce great and saintly men and women. Many of its unsung clergy were more than a credit to the teachings of Christ (you might like to read the *Parson's Tale* in this context) and the Church's central mission.

As with all such institutions you need to distinguish between its message, and the men who use, abuse, manipulate and distort that message. You may not agree with its beliefs but you must take account of its presence and influence on the work which Chaucer is presenting to us here. Apart from anything else, *The Canterbury Tales* are set against the background of a religious practice, the pilgrimage to Canterbury. Whilst such pilgrimages were often an excuse for many other things, they were as often undertaken in the true spirit of atonement for sin. You might like to consider the latter aspect in relation to what the Pardoner sells. Does he ever mention atonement, or sorrow for sin as a prerequisite for forgiveness? Would you consider that the message we get from the Pardoner is a negation of the pilgrimage which they are undertaking?

Death

In the social context of the Middle Ages, death was a fact of life which the medieval population was well acquainted with. The Black Death swept across Britain on three separate occasions in the 14th century, killing at least one third of the population. Medieval religious art is full of images of death, reflecting its pervasive presence, a presence from which modern man is largely insulated. For the majority of us, death has been sanitized, with all the 'uncomfortable' elements dealt with by professionals: doctors, undertakers and gravediggers for example. The grief is real enough, but the acquaintance with the face of death is less real. For medieval man, however, it was quite the opposite.

The *Pardoner's Prologue* and *Tale* has death as its centrepiece, not simply in the decay of man's mortal remains, but in the much more important matter of the soul. Again, your own view of man's nature and the existence or otherwise of God may well colour your reactions here, however, what is more relevant to this narrative is how medieval man viewed the matter. The state of the soul is something the Pardoner unequivocally dismisses as unimportant to him, and the flippant way in which he refers to the souls of the people he deceives, 'Though that hir soules goon a-blakeberyed!', would have greatly disturbed his medieval audience, striking as it does at the core and purpose of religious belief and practice.

You need to be conscious of the pervasive feeling of death which haunts the narrative, and note that the body's death is of note only in so far as it denotes the soul going to its final judgement.

Drunkenness

You may judge how the drunken state of the three rioters takes away any sense of them being in touch with reality. What is important here though, is that by getting into that state they deprive themselves of the power to reason, with fatal consequences not just for their earthly bodies but more importantly for their souls. In this respect then, drunkenness exemplifies an aspect of that sin against the Holy Spirit which wantonly rejects God's grace.

Be aware of the other examples of the sins that drunkenness leads men into. Was Lot's incest any worse than Herod's murder of St John the Baptist? (It is important to note that whereas the Bible does not actually give any suggestion that Herod was drunk, the Pardoner does suggest it.)

Drink also provides a structural link which runs throughout, serving as a backdrop to the Pardoner's narrative, from the Host's 'draughte of moyste and corny ale' through to the picture of the rioters sitting under a tree drinking poisoned wine. Is there a sense contained in that image of drink, that all drink is 'poisoned', and much as it leads to the rioters' death so too it may lead to the spiritual death of the soul?

Gambling

The many examples given of gambling, suggest the seriousness of this sin. Perhaps its central aspect is that in its dependence on chance or fortune, it acts as an image of man's denial of the responsibility he has for his own fate. Man is culpable, and therefore has the fate of his soul in his own hands.

Would you agree with the interpretation that the rioters, in their drunkenness, deny their capacity for reason, and when they give 'fortune' the credit for their finding gold, they reject their own culpability for action?

What do you feel the examples the Pardoner gives of gambling add to our understanding of the sin and its effects on man?

Gluttony

There is a real sense in which this sin encompasses both drunkenness and lechery, as well as its own more obvious connotation. The satisfaction of the sensory appetites of the body, to excess, has long been held to be a root cause for the fall of both man and empire. It speaks of man turning inward on himself, of being concerned only with 'self' to the exclusion of all others and, in the context of this sermon, to the exclusion of God.

The many references to cooking, eating, drunkenness and debauchery are the very antithesis of the Christian view which holds the body as being the temple of the soul. What degree of sin is being suggested in such an attack? Would you consider that the implications of the sin of gluttony are again a rejection of God's grace and a parody of the central act of Christian worship, the Eucharist?

Is the Pardoner a glutton? How would you justify your answer to this question? Do remember that perhaps we should not take a narrow and purely material view of gluttony in this context, but relate it to the religious beliefs of the time.

Haste

Perhaps the image of the Gadarene swine rushing to their deaths (Matthew 8:28) ought to spring to mind when we consider the swiftness of pace which accompanies the rioters' frantic search for Death.

Be aware of all those techniques that Chaucer employs to speed the pace of the narrative along and thereby create almost a sense of inevitability about the rioters' fate. The boy's measured words do not delay them, but merely spur them on their way. The Old Man, with all his experience and sagacity is brushed to one side, providing but a brief interval in their frenetic rush to Death and also adding to their desire for haste to discover Death which he assures them is 'in that grove'. Even the discovery of gold beyond their dreams hardly gives them pause for thought; note how their joy in its discovery is quickly subsumed in their fear of its loss, 'Men wolde seyn that we were theves stronge'. And so the narrative moves swiftly on to its inescapable conclusion.

From the 'go bet' addressed to the boy at the start of their tale, to the youngest rioter running around the streets getting his bottles filled with poison, they hardly have time to draw breath, and what breath they do draw is aimed at hastening the death of their fellows.

Apart from the boy's and the Old Man's narratives, the only other matters which slow the pace are the two sections which deal first with the two rioters' plot to kill their youngest companion, and his preparations to kill them. Would you agree that the final speed of their actual demise satisfactorily fulfils the impending sense of doom and inevitability which the preceding narrative has built up?

Holy Spirit

The Holy Spirit has a special place in the Church, especially with regard to the Church's mission to preach the Gospel of Christ. Early on in the *Prologue* the Pardoner uses the image of a dove to enable his audience to picture clearly how he goes about his work. The dove, of course, is the favourite way that the Holy Spirit is depicted in Christian art. Consider how the Pardoner usurps the pulpit for his own avaricious desires (in stark contrast to the fundamental mission of the Church which the pulpit effectively symbolizes – the preaching of the Gospel) and in doing so becomes symbolic of the rejection of the Holy Spirit.

The sin against the Holy Spirit which Christ mentioned (Matthew 12:31–32, Mark 3:28–29 and Luke 12:10) condemns the Pharisees for attributing Christ's work to the Devil. An interesting parallel may perhaps be seen in the Pardoner's contention that many a good sermon springs from evil intention. However, you might also like to consider the extent to which some of the events and characters which are depicted in the *Prologue* and *Tale* offend against those six sins generally enumerated by medieval theologians as being in a special way against the Holy Spirit: despair of salvation, presumption of God's mercy, attacking the accepted truths of the Church, envy of another's spiritual goodness, obstinacy in sin and final impenitence.

As mentioned elsewhere it is important to be aware of the centrality of religion in the lives of the medieval people. It was a far more pervasive influence on day-to-day living and thought of the mass of people, but one which we in the 20th century may find difficult at first to comprehend. On a cautionary note, do also be aware that, finally, it is a literary work which is being examined, not a religious tract – although perhaps there are elements of the latter in it?

Irony

The central irony of this whole narrative is that a sermon, condemning the sin of avarice, is being preached by a man whose only purpose in so preaching is to feed his own avaricious desires. The irony broadens to include the audience who listen to his words, and who, because of their own greed to secure their worldly goods and pleasures, are driven to purchase the Pardoner's worthless pardons and relics. The greatest irony of all is that the whole performance is presented in the language of religion and the saving of one's immortal soul, but the real underpinning desire is the acquisition and safe keeping of worldly goods.

In reading the *Prologue* and *Tale* many extensions of this central irony may be identified. There is the picture drawn of the Pardoner's effeminate appearance and the narrator's comment 'I trowe he were a geldyng or a mare', as compared to his own claim to 'have a joly wenche in every toun'; the sudden lack of interest the rioters show in Death when they discover the gold, which actually has the effect of hastening their search for Death, almost in spite of them; the Pardoner being reduced to speechlessness by the Host's riposte at the end of the *Tale*. Do be aware of these and other ironic touches which enliven the narrative and help to emphatically support the Pardoner's central theme.

Language

The English used by Chaucer is that which would be used by the educated Londoner of the time. Apart from the normal vocabulary of that group he occasionally uses words from other languages such as French, Italian and Latin.

Chaucer was well travelled and well read and such a wide use of vocabulary from other countries would not have been unusual. You should bear in mind that English as we know it now was then in the process of formation, with French gradually falling from favour and legal documents being written more and more in English instead of French. The influence of the Black Death should not be forgotten in this respect. Most teaching was done by friars who tended to live in institutions. As a group who lived in close proximity to each other they were thus hard hit by the plague; such decimation resulted in a lack of teachers, especially of French.

Other sources used by Chaucer were the vocabulary from other parts of England which in many ways was markedly different from Chaucer's English, and the spoken idiom of the time, much of which would not yet have found its way into books. Very occasionally Chaucer coined a new word himself.

In considering the *Pardoner's Tale* and *Prologue* it is important to note how the various registers of language not only reflect the people's speech, but also the content of the various sections and purposes of the narration. In doing so they provide a supporting image for the structural divisions (see notes under Rhetoric and Structure) of the *Prologue* and *Tale*.

References to domestic or village images, and religious symbolism, help to place and indicate possible interpretations of the author's intentions. Note how the forms of address to the pilgrim audience and the 'lewed' people are in marked contrast, perhaps also reflecting the Pardoner's attitude to them. Beware though, of being too dogmatic and simplistic in your initial appraisal of his attitude to his fellow pilgrims.

When the *Tale* begins, the first section of which is a declamation against the evils of drunkenness, lechery, gluttony and blasphemy, a whole flood of erudite, technical and what would be seen by his 'lewed' audience as 'high-flown' words are loosed on them. These words fit the lofty rhetoric and the references to Biblical and classical characters which the Pardoner uses to 'saffron' his message.

When the *Tale* proper begins and he turns to the adventure of the three rioters, the rhetoric disappears and we are left with a very down-to-earth narrative. This is reflected in both the simple sentence constructions used by most characters and in the lack of the previous specialist or technical vocabulary which supported the rhetoric. Note the contrast between the Old Man's speech and that of the rioters.

With the deaths of the three rioters there is a sudden return to the rhetoric—why? Note how the Pardoner also returns to previous modes of address as when he refers to the pilgrims and the 'lewed' people.

Do you think there is a certain irony in the Host picking up the Pardoner's reference to the 'soun' produced by the 'belle of dung and corruption' and giving a very effective example of it in his response to the Pardoner's jibe? What is its effect on the Pardoner, the master of rhetoric?

Old Man

The Old Man is the most enigmatic character in the narrative. That very enigma has spawned innumerable conclusions as to his identity and function. Is he God's agent of mercy whose purpose the rioters totally misread and therefore disregard; Death, in person, pointing the rioters towards their fate; the personification of age and wisdom; the Wandering Jew who, having offended God, is condemned to wander the earth forever? There are many other suggestions, apart from the rioters' own judgement on him that he is Death's spy.

Despite all these theories he remains a puzzle, though we can begin to come to some tentative conclusions if we consider his function in the story, as well as what he knows and does.

Would you consider that there is a link between him and the boy, both of whom make reference to their 'mother'? Could this be Holy Mother Church as it is so often described in religious literature? There are other similarities between them; for example their mode of address to the rioters and the fact that both seem to be in possession of knowledge about the likely fate of the rioters. Do they represent youth and age, on the one hand pure and unsullied and on the other world weary but resigned to the will of God, both in stark contrast to the three rioters? It would seem possible to draw a contrast between the Pardoner and the Old Man, the former in his rejection of God and the latter in his acceptance of God's will.

Does the Old Man know what Death is and where it is to be found? Or does he merely recognize in the rioters their lack of spirituality and, because of his experience of the world, is able to foresee the inevitable outcome of their discovery of gold?

What is the death that the Old Man looks for, a physical thing or something else, less tangible? What does he know about death and its consequences?

The mystery of the Old Man's persona creates many questions but no concrete answers. What is your opinion, and, equally as important, why do you hold it?

Pardoner

To some extent the Pardoner exemplifies two passages from the Bible that he *fails* to quote.

> 'For what shall it profit a man, if he shall gain the
> whole world, and lose his own soul?' (Mark 5:36)

> 'Man shall not live by bread alone, but by every word that
> proceedeth out of the mouth of God.' (Matthew 4:4)

How, if at all, does the first quotation highlight the central conflict in the message of the Pardoner, and the second his negation of God's word?

Again, we need to refer to the context of the *Tale*, a pilgrimage, and the part played by religion in the affairs of man during the Middle Ages. The religious background to the *Tale* and its overt, religious content must form a large part of our considerations when we assess the character and rôle of the Pardoner in the *Prologue* and *Tale*. However, that said, we must also step outside the purely religious context if we are to make judgements about the man's character and function in the narrative and the literary quality of his presentation.

The historical evidence for the evil practices of pardoners is very clear, as the following passage from *The Oxford Petition* of 1414 indicates:

> 'Although not in holy orders, they preach publicly, and pretend falsely that they
> have full powers of absolving both living and dead alike from punishment and
> guilt, along with other blasphemies, by means of which they plunder and seduce
> the people, and in all probability drag them down with their own persons to the
> infernal regions, by affording them frivolous hope and an audacity to commit sin.'

(Muriel Bowden, *A Commentary on the Canterbury Tales*. Quoted in *The Pardoner's Tale*, ed. Dewey R Faulkner, published by Prentice Hall.)

It is almost conceivable that in drawing up that petition the character of Chaucer's Pardoner was to the front of its authors' minds! Have they misrepresented him in any way?

Chaucer's Pardoner is a very complex character. From the description of his physical attributes and the author's implied view of his character in the *General Prologue*, you might imagine that we were about to be presented with a grossly overblown caricature without any real wit and presence. The final picture however, is very different. From the moment he begins his sermon, the other promise contained in the *General Prologue* is fulfilled, 'He was in chirche a noble ecclesiaste'. In this contrast between the man's appearance and his 'act', do we see reflected the irony of his sermon and the purpose behind it?

The Commentary explores in some detail the complex issues of the Pardoner and his narrative but it may be useful here to consider several questions. What is his purpose in freely admitting to his audience the purpose of his 'gaude' and 'false japes'? It could be to gain their confidence and thus lull them into a false sense of security, but to what purpose? The process of boasting about his avarice and the means he uses to achieve it, would apparently militate against the possibility of his success in that area. But is he actually attempting to exploit his fellow pilgrims or is he here the superb actor who, for the first time, can give a performance which is *not* directed at gaining other's money but at demonstrating the superlative mastery of his art? Is it possible that he can so effectively preach against the evils of avarice and yet remain untouched by his own words? Do be sensitive to the questions and problems of interpreting the character of the Pardoner as you investigate the *Prologue* and *Tale*.

Rhetoric

In Chaucer's time the art of preaching was a highly developed skill. It formed an important part of Church services and was a crucial means of teaching people about religious beliefs and duties. It was not, however, restricted to inside the church; the art of the sermon reached into the market-place and great houses of the time.

There was a well-tried formula for the method of delivering a sermon, and medieval audiences would have expected the *Pardoner's Prologue* and *Tale* to follow them. However, whilst Chaucer has here deviated from the strict formula, he has retained many of its elements, and his audience would have recognized them as such.

The Pardoner is quite open about his techniques – witness his declaration that he 'saffrons' his talk with Latin with the sole intention of thereby impressing his audience. Be aware of how carefully he establishes his credibility with the poor people by a nicely balanced introduction to his credentials, references to the Bible, a display of his wares and the good things that can come from them – at a price. Note how he plays on religious emotions and more particularly on people's avarice, an avarice made all the more sharp by the very uncertainties of their lives, subject as they were to the vagaries of the weather, disease, and their lords and masters.

An examination of the actual techniques the Pardoner uses to convey his message, influence his audience, and produce the desired result – money – will throw light on many aspects of his character, not least of which is the calculated way in which he goes about his task of fleecing the poor. That knowledge should also lead you on to a consideration of how culpable he is for his actions, the state of his soul and perhaps the speed with which he is pursuing 'death'.

Rioters

To what extent would you consider that in the tale of the three rioters we have the Pardoner's own life writ large, but at a much faster pace? Do the rioters exemplify all those sins which we might lay at the Pardoner's door, as well as those contained in the digression he makes before actually delivering his *Tale*?

Recognize what their drunkenness does to their ability to reason and the arrogant foolhardiness it leads them into. Notice how they fail to recognize the reality which is Death, even when they hear of the death of one of their own fellows and the news that some one thousand inhabitants have recently been slain by him. To the medieval audience, accustomed as they were to the visitation and ravages of plagues, such a blindness would have been almost incomprehensible.

Their treatment of the Old Man, their constant blasphemy, and the ever increasing pace of their rush to find Death all help to throw light on their characters. Can we actually consider them as individuals or should we see them as representing a wider view of man out of spiritual harmony with God? Why are none of them named?

Would you agree that they parody Christ in their mission to slay Death? His mission after all was to die for man in order to rise again for the salvation of man: the rioters wish to slay Death to avenge their fellow man. The Commentary considers other possible images that they represent, but you should also look out for related themes and images to see whether or not you would agree with such readings of the narrative.

Sin

Would you accept that the business of the Pardoner is to bring pardons to the people, but one of the central ironies is that instead of pardon he brings sin? Does the rioters' tale give us a parallel image of this? They sought to kill Death, and found gold instead, but the gold did not bring happiness, it brought death. What did the poor people seek from the Pardoner, and what did they gain?

The exact mode of sin is not important, what is important is what it does – which is to offend God, and its result – that is the destruction of God's grace in the soul.

In the Middle Ages the population were far more conscious of the concept of sin and its affect on the soul. The belief in man's fall from grace, of being born into the state of 'original sin', and the implications of such matters for the quest for eternal happiness in Heaven were a reality to medieval man. The visitations of the plague on the country were seen as the 'wages' of sin. However, it was not just the corruption of the body that sin brought, but the corruption of the soul. It is in the latter context that the narrative explores the multiplicity of sins that the Pardoner speaks of and exemplifies.

Structure

As may be adduced from the comments under 'Rhetoric', the *Prologue* and *Tale* are very carefully structured. There is a process whereby the Pardoner introduces his theme and himself, and then, bit by bit, builds upon that information, amplifying its form and meaning.

The structure of the narrative is inextricably bound up with the Pardoner's rhetorical techniques and many of the comments made under that section also apply here.

Note how the structure of the narrative supports the Pardoner's purposes and is carefully designed to ensure that the attention of a listening audience is kept. Equally be aware of how he weaves the sermon he gives to the poor people with a parallel dissertation to his pilgrim audience. The narrative structure is therefore working on three interrelated levels: the poor people, the pilgrim audience, and the audience to whom the entire *Prologue* and *Tale* would have been read.

If you read your text attentively you will easily discern the different registers of expression both in the way he addresses his audiences and the language used. Note how those features reflect the divisions in the narrative. You ought to be familiar with the major divisions into which the narrative falls, and the associated sub-divisions. If you read it closely, all are very clearly indicated in the text.

Finding your way around the commentary

Each page of the commentary gives the following information:

1 A quotation from the start of each line on which a comment is made, so that you can easily locate the right place in your text.

2 A series of comments, explaining, interpreting, and drawing your attention to important incidents, characters and aspects of the text.

3 For each comment, headings to indicate the important characters, themes, and ideas dealt with in the comment.

4 For each heading, a note of the comment numbers in this guide where the previous or next comment dealing with that heading occurred.

Thus you can use this commentary section in the following ways.

1 Turn to that part of the commentary dealing with the lines you are perhaps revising for a class discussion or essay. Read through the comments in sequence, referring all the time to the text, which you should have open before you. The comments will direct your attention to all the important things of which you should take note.

2 Take a character or topic from the list on page 28. Note the comment number next to it. Turn to that comment in this guide, where you will find the first of a number of comments on your chosen topic. Study it, and the appropriate part of your text to which it will direct you. Note the comment number in this guide where the next comment for your topic occurs and turn to it when you are ready. Thus, you can follow one topic right through your text.

For example, you want to examine in depth the 'avarice' theme of the *Tale*. Turning to the topic list, you will find that this theme first occurs in comment 19. On turning to comment 19 you will discover a zero (0) in the place of the previous reference (because this is the first time that it has occurred) and the number 21 for the next reference. You now turn to comment 21 and find that the previous comment number is 19 (from where you have just been looking) and that the next reference is to comment 33, and so on throughout the text.

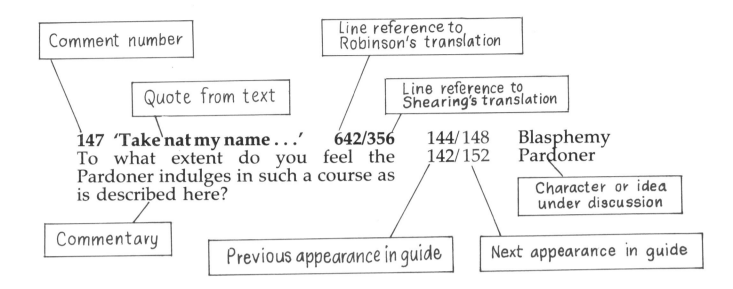

Characters	*Comment no:*		**Topics**	*Comment no:*
Boy	160		Audience	1
Old Man	182		Avarice	19
Pardoner	1		Background	2
Rioters	97		Bible	46
			Blasphemy	22
			Church	18
			Death	155
			Drunkenness	10
			Gambling	136
			Gluttony	10
			Haste	159
			Holy Spirit	61
			Irony	1
			Language	20
			Rhetoric	20
			Sin	2
			Structure	28

Commentary

Introduction to the Pardoner from the General Prologue

1 With hym ther rood . . .   669

We have here the first ironic reference to the Pardoner. You will be able to judge at a later stage just how much of a 'gentil' he was. He later addresses his fellow pilgrims by the title 'Lordynges', and you might like to consider whether you feel he is being ironic and if he views them with the same somewhat jaundiced eye as they have for him!

2 Of Rouncivale, his . . .   670

The contemporary audience would have made the connection between the Hospital of the Blessed Virgin Mary at Charing Cross and its mother house at Rouncivale in Navarre. Is it perhaps just coincidence that two lines later the Pardoner should sing what was presumably a song of uncertain propriety 'Com hider, love, to me' just after being linked with a house dedicated to the Blessed Virgin? Does it forewarn us of the uncertain nature of his character? Certainly, he evidences more than hints of lechery in this introduction and also in his *Prologue*. You will note the recurrence of this sin in the characters of the three rioters in the *Tale* proper.

3 Of Rouncivale, his . . .   670

It is interesting to note that in 1379, the Hospital and Chapel of St Mary Rouncivale, its buildings and lands, were seized by Richard II because of abuses in alms collecting which were associated with it. They were restored in 1383. However, in 1387 it achieved notoriety again following a scandal involving the unauthorized sale of pardons.

No doubt Chaucer's audience would make the connection between those events and this Pardoner who apparently has a close affinity to that institution.

4 That streight was . . .   671

No doubt the Pardoner would have us believe that he came straight from Rome, the centre of Christianity, largely because he gains importance in the eyes of others from such a claim; it would also help give credence to his claim to have 'Bulles of popes' in his possession. To an extent, the next few lines comment on such a claim. Would a person such as is described in this introduction actually bother to make the dangerous and time-consuming journey to Rome, for some scraps of paper that could be forged anywhere?

5 Ful loude he soong . . .   672

The song he sings, of which we hear but a snatch, indicates that this Pardoner is very much a wordly man, a view that will be confirmed in a number of places throughout the narrative. Can you think of any?

6 Ful loude he soong . . .   672

The introduction to the Pardoner creates for the audience a number of contradictions which you might feel the need to resolve at a later stage. Equally, the mere fact of there being such seeming contradictions leaves us in some doubt about the veracity of the Pardoner's words and creates a satisfying ambience for his *Prologue* and *Tale*.

The contrast between his and the Summoner's voice is our first indication of what the Pardoner may sound like. However, as already mentioned, this will be one of those matters which raises feelings of doubt. Bear in mind how later in this introduction the Pardoner's voice is described, and then in the *Prologue* to his *Tale* see if you feel there is some difference between description and reality, and which is which.

7 This Somonour bar . . .   673

Is there a hint here, in the contrast mentioned between the two voices? Are we to draw comparisons and inferences between the overt masculinity of the Summoner's 'stif bourdon' – deep bass voice – and an effeminacy in the Pardoner's voice?

6/8	Pardoner

8 This Pardoner hadde heer . . .   675

The description of the Pardoner's hair is the first reference to physical appearance. Five lines give us some detail – why do you think Chaucer spent so much time on it? In medieval times the study of physiognomy (the relationship between a man's character and his physical appearance) was much respected. Such hair as Chaucer has just described was taken to be a sign of both effeminacy and cunning. We have already commented on the former and you should look for other suggestions of his lack of masculinity as you read the *General Prologue* and then the *Pardoner's Prologue* and *Tale*. The cunning of the Pardoner will be well exemplified as the story unfolds.

3/9	Background
7/9	Pardoner

9 But hood, for jolitee . . .   680

It was unusual for the Pardoner to ride bare-headed, and Chaucer comments that he did it for 'jolitee' and saw himself as being with the latest fashion. You might like to consider whether such a desire and practice on the Pardoner's part was in keeping with his supposed mission in life.
Is there an ironic comment here in 'Hym thoughte . . .'? The Pardoner thinks of himself as being fashionable, but does anyone else? To what extent does the description so far tell us something about the Pardoner's character, particularly about how he views himself? Could the word 'dischevele' suggest how he really looked in the eyes of his companions?

8/10	Background
8/10	Pardoner

10 Swiche glarynge eyen . . .   684

The glaring eyes were looked upon as a distinct sign of the owner's gluttony, drunkenness and lecherous nature (the latter has already been dwelt upon briefly when referring to his song). The sins of gluttony and drunkenness feature largely in the *Pardoner's Tale* and *Prologue* and we are forewarned of them here in the description of the Pardoner.

9/11	Background
0/23	Drunkenness
0/25	Gluttony
9/11	Pardoner

11 A vernycle hadde . . .   685

The wearing of a 'vernycle', a copy of the cloth that St Veronica was believed to have wiped Christ's face with as He carried His cross to Calvary, and on which was believed to be the imprint of Christ's features, typifies much about the Pardoner. Perhaps surprisingly (though not really) there is no attempt on his part to suggest it was the original, but as you will see later it is suggestive of the value he attaches to such relics.

10/12	Background
10/12	Pardoner

12 Bretful of pardoun . . .   687
The practice of granting indulgences, or remission of punishment for sin, was the source of much of the Pardoner's income, his stock-in-trade. Such proof of his rights to carry on his occupation was therefore of great importance to him. That they should be thought to come from Rome would give him even greater status in the eyes of those to whom he sold them.

13 A voys he hadde . . .   688
The goat has long been synonymous with lechery, but in addition, Chaucer here comments on the Pardoner's voice. This is the second reference to the subject, and is one of some importance, for the Pardoner earns his living through the effectiveness of his preaching. Is this imaging of his voice as being like a goat something which we should take literally or as perhaps a suggestion of something to do with the content of what he preaches? Does it also contribute towards the complete picture of the man which Chaucer is building for us and against which, and as a result of, we will be able to make much clearer judgements about the man and his character?

14 Ne berd hadde . . .   689
The lack of a beard on a grown man, especially when it was customary to grow one, plus the suggestion that his face was unnaturally smooth adds to the growing suspicion that the Pardoner was not as manly as his words and actions attempt to proclaim. Do you think he was conscious of being effeminate and thus knowingly tried to overcome it? Is there perhaps the possibility that the conflict within him caused by a male form and an effeminate nature is the root cause of the excesses in which he indulges in the pursuance of his own wealth?

Don't be tempted to spend too much time on the psychological approach to the origins of the Pardoner's evil ways. The Chaucerian audience would have had a very robust attitude towards seeming homosexuality; their religious convictions would also lead them to see such a man as being separated from God and his Church, as indeed the Pardoner will prove to be.

15 I trowe he were . . .   691
Do you think that the brutal force of this statement has something in common with the Host's reaction to the Pardoner at the end of the *Tale*? (See lines 946 *et seq.*) Certainly, when taken together with the comments already given about the Pardoner's character and form, we can be left in little doubt that if he was not actually homosexual, then he certainly exhibited all the gross faults and contradictions which the medieval audience would have attributed to and associated with such a person, and in particular the moral degeneracy of the man.

The apparent contradictions about the Pardoner's character have been commented on before. We now have a picture before us: that of an effeminate man, exemplifying the rejection of God's grace which grievous sin causes and of which the Pardoner is a personification. This is further amplified when we consider that the method by which he gains his wealth, preaching in God's name, is that same method by which the Apostles spread God's word.

16 But of his craft . . .   692
Could there be, from 'Berwyk into Ware', ever another creature like the one

just described? The gross picture painted of the man's appearance and his associated characteristics will now be enhanced with some choice details of the deceits he practises on the common people, deceits which will find their detailed parallels in the Pardoner's *Prologue*.

17 But of his craft . . .   692

For the Pardoner the concept of success is measured by the extent to which he can successfully cheat other people out of their money.

16/18   Pardoner

18 For in his male . . .   694

Like a magician's hat, in the Pardoner's travelling bag, or male, was a whole collection of dubious relics with which to work wonders on his audiences' purses. The people of that time had a great devotion to numerous saints, and the possession of associated relics would have been of great help to the Pardoner. The obviously outrageous nature of his claims for the 'relics' he possesses gives us an indication of the lengths to which he is prepared to go.

0/86   Church
17/19   Pardoner

19 A povre person . . .   702

Without doubt there were great malpractices in the Church during the Middle Ages. Equally there was great holiness, and the Parson, as may be seen from the *Parson's Tale*, despite his poverty and ignorance was as holy and well motivated as the Pardoner was the very opposite.

0/21   Avarice
14/29   Background
18/20   Pardoner

That the Pardoner could extract as much money in one day as the Parson would get in two months, indicates both the mastery that the Pardoner had of his craft and the gross extent of his own avarice. This is always assuming, of course, that his estimation of his earnings is to be unquestioningly believed!

20 And thus, with feyned . . .   705

There is a reference later in the *Prologue* to the misuse to which the Pardoner puts the pulpit. The almost lighthearted feeling conveyed by 'flaterye and japes' makes for a strong contrast with the 'apes' that he makes of the Parson and people.

0/33   Language
19/21   Pardoner
0/29   Rhetoric

21 But trewely to tellen . . .   707

How 'truly' are we being told here? Can you list the anomalies between the picture of the Pardoner as just drawn and the image here presented of him being in church a 'noble ecclesiaste'? Is he such a consummate actor that he can overcome his lank yellow hair, his glaring eyes, and voice as 'smal as a goot', a voice which can read a lesson and sing an offertory such that he would 'wynne silver'?

19/33   Avarice
1/26   Irony
20/24   Pardoner

Is there a suggestion implied here that for the Pardoner to make such a great success against the disabilities outlined by Chaucer, he must effectively preach his avaricious message to the already converted? You might like to bear this possibility in mind when you read the *Prologue* to the *Pardoner's Tale*. When you consider that the whole art of the Pardoner really rests on a lie (he preaches against avarice in pursuit of his own avarice), one should not be unduly dismayed by what may seem to be contradictory images of the man in Chaucer's and the Pardoner's presentations.

The Words of the Host

22 Oure Hooste gan . . .   287
The Host's introduction to the *Pardoner's Tale* comes just at the end of the *Physician's Tale* and presents us with the Host looking for a tale which will act as a relief from the harrowing nature of the tragedy just heard. It is perhaps appropriate that his first words should centre our attention on the blasphemous outpourings which will be so important in the Pardoner's narrative. Would you agree that his 'by nayles and by blood' reflects a central theme of the *Pardoner's Tale* in that it suggests the Cross and Christ's sacrifice on it, a sacrifice that was meant to save man and conquer 'death'?

0/144   Blasphemy

23 'Or elles a draughte . . .'   315
This reference to the need for a drink of ale foreshadows the concern we shall see displayed in the *Pardoner's Prologue* and *Tale* about the sin of drunkenness. It is a theme which will be immediately picked up by the Pardoner.

10/25   Drunkenness

24 'Telle us som myrthe . . .'   319
Is there a clue here to the Pardoner's intention in his tale? Does he see this as an opportunity to have some fun at his audience's expense?

1/30   Audience
21/26   Pardoner

25 'I wol bothe drynke . . .'   322
Perhaps the character of the Pardoner is further indicated here in his desire to first fill his belly, before telling his tale.

23/89   Drunkenness
10/43   Gluttony

26 But right anon . . .   323
If the introduction to the Pardoner in the *General Prologue* were not enough to warn us of the Pardoner's character, then the reaction of the 'gentils' here ought to make it plain what they think is likely to come from his mouth.

Their desire to be told 'som moral thyng' will, however, be complied with, but not quite in the way they expected.

21/38   Irony
24/27   Pardoner

27 'I graunte ywis . . .'   328
Why might you agree that the Pardoner really requires no time to think about a suitable 'moral thyng'? Is he more concerned about getting himself a drink with which he perhaps needs to fortify himself as he prepares for yet another performance?

26/29   Pardoner

The Pardoner's Prologue

28 'Lordynges', quod he . . .   329/43
The Pardoner here introduces his audience to the fact that he preaches in church, an announcement which is made with an air of confidence and brooks no surprised comment or dissent from his audience. You might like to bear in mind here the description of him in the introduction of the *General Prologue*.

0/34   Structure

Having made a brief comment on the quality of his sermon delivery, he then announces his theme; all in all it is a very competent introduction to himself and his sermon, briefly and clearly done.

---

29 'Lordynges', quod he . . .   329/43
In this first line the Pardoner seems to assume certain rights and status which were not necessarily his. Here he effectively lays claim to the right to preach from church pulpits almost with the authority of an ordained priest.

19/39   Background
27/30   Pardoner
20/36   Rhetoric

Chaucer's audience will have been well aware of the outrageous behaviour for which pardoners were well known in the Middle Ages. Originally they were quite specifically forbidden to preach, but with time attitudes and rules changed. Whether this particular Pardoner had such rights as he obviously assumes is a moot point; what is not in doubt is the arrogance with which he here lays claim to the right to preach in church, and indeed later, to other rights which were most definitely restricted to ordained priests.

This proprietary attitude to the pulpit will be repeated later in the *Prologue* when he refers to 'my pulpet' (1.391/105). Almost certainly he is trying to impress his audience of fellow pilgrims, just as he attempts to do when using Latin on the ignorant folk to whom he sells his pardons and fake relics. Whatever the truth of the implied claims, they would immediately arouse a response in the mind of Chaucer's medieval audience.

---

30 I peyne me to . . .   330/44
He is suggesting that his voice is loud and clear as a bell. This statement is one that the reader who is familiar with the *Prologue* will see as perhaps being a little confusing. In the Pardoner's introduction in the *Prologue* to *The Canterbury Tales* his voice is described as being 'as smal as hath a goot' (1.688). Is there a great gulf between the reality of what the Pardoner is and what he wants his audience to believe, or is his 'hauteyn' voice a tribute to the consummate acting skills of the man? Yet again, we have questions raised in our minds.

24/38   Audience
29/31   Pardoner

How might his audience of fellow pilgrims react to his description of his voice and the reality of the sound they hear as he speaks to them? What was the reality? Throughout the *Prologue* and *Tale* we see the Pardoner quite calmly insulting the intelligence of his audience by blatantly telling them of his *'cupiditas'* and then shamelessly attempting to blandish them to the same effect. Does he succeed?

There might also be an element of self-deception here. Does the Pardoner believe that his voice will 'rynge . . . out as round as . . . a belle' – and does it? Either way it adds another piece of information to the developing picture of his character.

---

31 For I kan al . . .   332/46
Well practised in his trickery, the Pardoner sees no reason to vary his story or style. He knows the weaknesses of the simple people he deals with and how best to part them from their money. Be aware of how already he exudes a noticeable degree of confidence (and pleasure?) in his abilities – or perhaps arrogance would be a more apt description of his attitude as so far witnessed.

30/32   Pardoner

---

32 My theme is alwey . . .   333/47
The Pardoner's theme is always the same; effectively he has but one tale to

31/35   Pardoner

tell and he introduces it in the next line. However, you will need to be aware that the tale he is about to tell is a 'cap that will fit many heads', not least of them being the Pardoner himself.

---

33 *Radix malorum* . . .   334/47

'The love of money is the root of all evils'; there are two aspects to this Latin 'tag' of which you should be aware. As the theme of his tale, it most obviously applies to the Pardoner himself, indeed, later in the *Prologue* he defines exactly what he means by 'cupiditas' (1.400/114). Check what it is. In line 344/58 he makes a comment about using Latin; consider whether there is the same intention in its use here.

21/45   Avarice
20/41   Language

---

34 First I pronounce . . .   335/50

Here the Pardoner introduces the format of his sermon, together with brief details of the precautions he takes to save himself from any interruptions and the stock-in-trade of warrants and relics he carries around with him, amplifying the information found in the first few lines of the *Prologue*.

28/47   Structure

---

35 First I pronounce . . .   335/50

The Pardoner has a very carefully worked out routine for presenting his tale. One of his primary concerns is to ensure that he establishes his 'credentials' and the right to sell indulgences. That he should feel the need to do this suggests pardoners were not well thought of and also that he was perhaps mindful of his own personal safety.

(Note the description of him in the *Prologue* to *The Canterbury Tales* and the comments made earlier in this guide as to the possibility of his being homosexual. Why might this have proved likely to increase the insecurity of his position when it came to attempting to exploit the people to whom he desired to sell indulgences and spurious cures from 'holy' relics?)

32/37   Pardoner

---

36 And thanne my bulles . . .   336/51

The official documents with a seal attached, giving the Pardoner authority to 'ply his trade', are the first things he flourishes at his audience. Whether 'Oure lige lordes seel' is that of the Pope or of the local Bishop is not clear, but the Pardoner's license or a forgery thereof was the key to his activities. Once his credibility on that count was established, then the rag-bag of 'relics' which he would later produce would obviously gain credence from his status as Pardoner.

29/42   Rhetoric

---

37 That shewe I first . . .   338/52

The first concern of the Pardoner, 'my body to warente' is quite shamelessly stated. His 'cupiditas' is not so overwhelming as to interfere with his concern for his personal safety!

35/38   Pardoner

---

38 That no man be . . .   339/53

The Pardoner is a real expert at his job. He establishes his credentials, secures his personal safety, and ensures that there can be no interference from 'preest ne clerk'. It is a very cold and calculated performance in which he indulges.

The barefaced effrontery of the man is evidenced in his next comment that

30/45   Audience
26/49   Irony
37/39   Pardoner

he is about 'Cristes holy werk'. In fact it is the Pardoner's work that he is about – not Christ's! Yet there is a great irony here which involves not just the Pardoner but also his usual audience, and one that points to the huge contradiction between what he preaches and what he does, and between what his 'lewed' audience in purchasing his pardons and worthless relics are attempting to achieve.

Later, you will need to judge whether it is holiness and oneness with God that they seek, or earthly security derived from productive flocks and crops, together with matrimonial peace – whatever the reality.

39 And after that . . .   341/55

Why might we expect on the evidence so far that 'tales' is also what the audience should expect his 'Bulles of popes and of cardynales, . . .' etc. to be, and with as much reliance to be placed on them? Certainly the forgery of such documents was common practice in the Middle Ages and there are many recorded complaints from Church officials about such occurrences.

29/40   Background
38/41   Pardoner

40 Bulles of popes . . .   342/56

There is no clear evidence for the exact date of the composition of the *Pardoner's Prologue* and *Tale*. The *Tales* were written between 1387 and 1400, and it is thought that the Pardoner's was probably not among Chaucer's earlier stories. Some evidence suggests that a possible date for its composition was about 1390.

39/42   Background

The relevance of this comment concerns the reference to 'popes' – in the plural. It is quite possible that here the Pardoner is being cynical, flourishing warrants from several Popes when in practice he could only have had a 'bulle' from one Pope (obviously, there were many cardinals and bishops who could have given him a warrant). It would certainly be in character for him to produce, as evidence of his right to be a Pardoner, documents from seemingly contradictory sources.

However, you need to be aware that in 1378 there occurred in the Church what is known as The Great Schism. In that year Urban VI, an Italian, was elected Pope. Later in the same year a group of cardinals declared his election invalid and elected another Pope, Clement VII, who took up residence in Avignon during 1379. Thus there were two 'Popes' and tremendous confusion and rivalries throughout Christendom.

The Schism continued under their successors and it was not until 1417 that it came to an end, following the resignation of Gregory III, the deposition of Jonn XXIII and the eventual condemnation of Benedict XIII as a heretic and schismatic, with just one Pope, Martin V, in charge of the Church. (This list of 'unsatisfactory' Popes gives some idea of the degree of politicking that was going on and the unsavoury political and personal pressures that could be brought to bear on a Pope's election.) Could it be that this reference to 'popes' is a reference on Chaucer's part to yet further evidence of the confusion then apparent in the Church?

41 And in Latyn . . .   344/58

As previously suggested, and now confirmed, the Pardoner uses Latin to suggest to his gullible audience that he is a learned man. Has he already started to use the same line of trickery with the other pilgrims to whom he is relating this story? (Note the Latin 'tag' he has already used in line 336/48.) The reader will perhaps recognize this as the beginning of the Pardoner's outrageous openness in freely admitting the trickery he is to indulge in when parting his audience from their money.

33/42   Language
39/45   Pardoner

42 And in Latyn . . .   344/58

To recognize the importance of the Latin tag in the Pardoner's and his audience's minds you need to be aware of the part played by Latin in the culture of the Middle Ages. Unlike now, it was a living language, indeed, effectively the international language of the time. All church services were conducted in it (only in the 1960s was the use of the vernacular introduced into services in the Catholic Church), virtually all religious and philosophical writings were in Latin and it was also the language of universities and schools. Not until the late Middle Ages when Dante wrote in Italian and Chaucer in English did other languages supersede Latin as the language of literature.

Given this background and the fact that the majority of the population was totally illiterate, you may understand why the Pardoner considered, probably rightly, that the occasional Latin tag would help convince his audience of the strength and veracity of his claims. You will note that he does not use Latin frequently, but some of his vocabulary is very 'latinate', and no doubt also, the other 'high-sounding' words he uses all add to the effect he is trying to create in order to impress his audience.

43 To saffron with my . . .   345/59

Saffron is used in cooking as a flavouring and colourant. This metaphor foreshadows the introduction of a major theme of the *Prologue* and *Tale*, that of gluttony. His use of Latin, which is the 'saffron' of his discourse, is to 'stire' – note the continuation of the cooking metaphor – his audience to the right frame of mind, one where they will respond to his blandishments and the promises of his worthless relics. The Pardoner is playing the oldest trick in the book by using religious emotions to extract money from his audience.

You might look for parallels in our modern world, especially amongst some of the more unscrupulous evangelists and 'fringe' religions to be found in Western society. It is quite obvious that the stirring of his audience to 'devocioun' has but one purpose, and you ought at this stage to be able to easily identify that purpose!

44 Thanne shewe I forth . . .   347/61

Note the care with which the Pardoner has gone about his business. Not least of his concerns is the presentation of his goods, already seen in the flourishing of diverse 'bulles'. Here he displays his wares in receptacles made of glass so that all may see, but not yet touch! Note also a few lines down how the sheep's shoulder bone is encased in metal.

45 Relikes been they . . .   349/63

To what extent are we being invited to admire the Pardoner's expertise as he here points out to his pilgrim audience something that should be obvious to them: that the poor people actually believe what the Pardoner is telling them? Is the reader, and his pilgrim audience being drawn in by Chaucer to identify with the Pardoner, to admire his cleverness and thus to lose their own sense of reality and ability to judge the man, his pardons and relics as frauds? To what extent do you think the poor people believe merely because of their own overriding avarice?

You ought to consider, that much as the Pardoner is to be held in contempt for the avarice he displays, how successful he might have been if the poor people in their own way and for their own more modest aims were not also overcome by avarice. Yet do be careful in making judgements about the poor. Their experience of life was in stark contrast to that of the Pardoner, who had about him the aura – whether honestly so or not is irrelevant here – of the Church, which wielded such a huge influence over the lives of the people in the Middle Ages.

46 Which that was of . . .   351/65

There is no absolute identification of who the 'hooly Jewes' was, though he is often taken to be Jacob, one of the great patriarchs of the Old Testament. (See Genesis 30:31–43.)

0/50	Bible

47 'Goode men,' I seye . . .   352/66

So far we have seen a brief (six lines) introduction amplified, giving some detail as to the 'window-dressing' which helps to sell the Pardoner's 'goods'. Now he proceeds to give an example of how he would tackle the actual sermon. Note, so far then, the logical progression by which the Pardoner carefully outlines his technique; such care will be evidenced throughout the *Prologue* and *Tale*.

34/62	Structure

48 'Goode men,' I seye . . .   352/66

With the introduction of this quotation, the Pardoner neatly bridges the gap between the 'tale' he is telling his pilgrim audience and the attempt he is to make at turning them into objects of his 'cupiditas'. From this moment on he is the Pardoner in 'full flight' as it were. And whilst on one level we know that he is describing his technique, would you agree that on another level he is actually attempting here to practise his art?

45/52	Pardoner
44/50	Rhetoric

49 If cow, or calf . . .   354/68

You will appreciate that the Middle Ages was based upon a rural economy. A peasant's richest possession would be his livestock. The Pardoner well knows this and his first appeal is therefore to his audience's own desire to keep their wordly goods safe. The irony here of course is that the Pardoner is using *their* cupidity to further his own, though one has perhaps rather more sympathy with his audience than him.

45/50	Avarice
42/52	Background
38/67	Irony

50 If that the good-man . . .   361/75

There is nothing that quite enhances our satisfaction at obtaining a bargain as much as the belief that we are getting good value for money. Hence the Pardoner fuels his audience's expectations by further 'describing' the potency of water that has been in contact with his 'holy' bone. The mere drinking of such water will have the effect of ensuring the owner's beasts will multiply. Note also the implied underpinning of the Pardoner's claims from his use and reliance on 'facts' which one may assume are to be found in the Bible, something his audience most certainly would not have access to, or could have read if they did.

49/51	Avarice
46/105	Bible
48/51	Rhetoric

51 And, sires, also it . . .   366/80

Having satisfied his male audience's 'cupiditas' in their concern for their stock, the Pardoner now makes a quite ridiculous claim for his bone, a claim which again indicates his contempt for his audience's intelligence, and his very judicious assessment of what will help sell his wares to the wives sitting in the audience!

45/53	Audience
50/53	Avarice
50/53	Rhetoric

You might at this stage find it easier to judge the effectiveness of the

Pardoner's sales pitch if you just bear in mind for a moment the advertisements which appeared in Victorian newspapers offering ointments and other 'cures' whose supposed beneficial effects were constrained only by the limits of the manufacturers' imaginations. Quack medicine and the medicine man are not far removed from our Pardoner in intent, and he was dealing with a far more superstitious and easily influenced audience than the 'modern' conman, though the underlying human cupidity in each audience is of the same variety. (You might like to consider how many of the 'seven deadly sins' modern television advertising uses to exploit particular products.)

52 Al had she taken . . .   371/85
There is perhaps another intentional reference here by Chaucer to the illegal practices of many churchmen. Here the Pardoner suggests the priests were indulging in illicit sex. It was not unknown for priests to be married and over the centuries many a prelate of the Church made little attempt to disguise the existence of mistresses and illegitimate offspring. Apart from moral considerations, in the context of the Pardoner's tale to his fellow pilgrims it is rather a 'cheap' and uncalled-for remark and it says rather more about the Pardoner than it does about the clergy whom he so calmly maligns. If you have the time, you will be well rewarded if you read through the *Parson's Tale*, so as to gain a perspective of what a true priest could be like.

49/56	Background
48/56	Pardoner
13/55	Sin

53 Heere is a miteyn . . .   372/86
Having appealed to the desire of his audience to preserve their livestock and domestic harmony, the Pardoner now turns his attention to crops, and promises equal success in the multiplication of grain. Like any good salesman however, the Pardoner has left the price to be paid to the end, 'he offre pens or ellis grotes'. Without such an offering, all the Pardoner's promises are beyond reach. Has the Pardoner so far offered anything remotely to do with the saving of his audience's souls, or, at the very least, that would succour their wish for holiness? In this reference to the payment they will have to make we see linked the 'cupiditas' of both the Pardoner and his audience.

51/55	Audience
51/56	Avarice
51/54	Rhetoric

54 Goode men and wommen . . .   377/91
Having now introduced the monetary 'pill' which his audience may find difficult to swallow, the Pardoner proceeds to indulge in some calculated moral blackmail to persuade any waverers that their best course lies in paying 'pens' or 'grotes' for services.

53/55	Rhetoric

55 If any wight be . . .   378/92
Carefully note the content of the Pardoner's words over the next six lines, especially with regard to any wife that may have 'cuckolded her husband'. Which woman is going to admit, by not making use of the Pardoner's services, that she has cuckolded her husband? Is there a conflict here with the previous promise that water touched by his 'holy' bone could cure jealousy about a wife's adultery with another man? Is there an attempt to create mistrust and suspicion between man and wife in order to further his own cause?

53/57	Audience
54/56	Rhetoric
52/56	Sin

56 If any wight be . . .   378/92
Many of that group of sins known as the 'seven deadly sins' – pride, wrath, envy, lust, gluttony, avarice and sloth – are writ large in the *Pardoner's Tale* and *Prologue*. Would you consider that his audience are in danger here of falling into any of these sins? Which has the Pardoner himself so far demonstrated? Previously the Pardoner has addressed himself largely to the male sex, now he broadens his appeal by also calling upon 'any womman, be she yong or old'. He is not about to miss a trick when it comes to maximizing income. We shall later see the depths to which he will freely acknowledge he is prepared to sink in order to make a sale.

It is worth noting here that the Pardoner is also exploiting the Church's rulings about the granting of indulgences. These included amongst the preconditions for granting such an indulgence that it was necessary for the person to be in a state of grace. He should have no unabsolved mortal sin on his conscience. (Mortal sin was a grievous and knowing act against God, for example, the breaking of one of the Ten Commandments.) By challenging his audience to demonstrate they are not in mortal sin through the use of his services, he poses a real problem for these simple folk – you might like to bear this in mind when he later calls upon the Host to avail himself of the Pardoner's services.

52/59	Background
52/57	Pardoner
55/62	Rhetoric
55/64	Sin

57 And I assoille him . . .   387/101
The Pardoner completes his speech with an appeal once again to the authority of the 'papal bull' in his possession. The whole performance has been nicely calculated to appeal to his audience's baser instincts, backed up by the Pardoner's visual aids of relics and bulls. Can you now clearly set down the relationship between Pardoner and audience that has been created through his sermon; the means by which it was done and the emotions which have been aroused in the audience's minds?

55/61	Audience
56/59	Pardoner

58 By this gaude . . .   389/103
Now directly addressing his fellow pilgrims, the Pardoner lays bare the success of his trade and the fact that he has been plying it 'yeer by yeer'. A hundred marks is an enormous sum, a monument to the Pardoner's expertise and avarice. It also serves to indicate the extent to which the 'lewed peple' were willing to take advantage of his spurious offerings and says something of their 'cupiditas' as well.

53/63	Avarice

59 I stonde lyk a clerk . . .   391/105
The Pardoner was not a priest whose ministry included the preaching of Christ's Gospel, his remit was quite precisely defined, yet there is evidence enough here to see how the Pardoner abused his position. Note, 'my pulpet', the proprietary terminology which stresses the effrontery of the man and perhaps suggests the laxity of the Church authorities in dealing with the abuses which such pardoners perpetrated.

56/60	Background
57/60	Pardoner

60 And telle an hundred . . .   394/108
To what extent do you think the Pardoner is enjoying the telling of his story? The statement that he has a hundred such ways of extracting money from the 'lewed peple' suggests that he enjoys his work. What other evidence is there of such enjoyment in the *Prologue* and *Tale*? Note the unconcerned admittance contained in 'false japes'. Is the Pardoner an honest man? Be careful how you construct your answer to this question.

59/69	Background
59/61	Pardoner

There is sometimes a certain beguiling quality which might attract us to an 'honest' rogue. To what extent do you feel that while Chaucer is condemning the malpractices which the institution of pardoners by the Church has led to, he also demonstrates an admiration for the outright roguery and professional competence of the man? This is a question on which you might for a moment wish to reserve judgement!

---

61 Thanne peyne I me . . .   395/109
This image likening the Pardoner to a dove works on three levels.

First, the image of a dove in a barn centres his tale clearly amongst the peasantry of the time, and gives a beautifully clear image of his movements as he addresses his audience. It puts him clearly above his audience both physically, and, in his own mind, intellectually.

Next, take careful note of this description by the Pardoner of his physical presence and actions whilst telling his story. The man sees himself as a consummate actor, even to the extent of enjoying and glorying in his own performance.

Finally, there is an associated image here with which the medieval audience might well have drawn a connection, that of the dove as a symbol of the Holy Spirit, something for which the Pardoner with his trade in indulgences ought to have some concern. (The seven rays which are traditionally depicted as proceeding from the dove (or Holy Spirit) are a reference to his 'seven gifts': wisdom, understanding, counsel, fortitude, knowledge, righteousness, and fear of the Lord. How many do you think apply to the Pardoner or his audience? You might also like to bear in mind their contrast with the 'seven deadly sins' mentioned previously in comment 56.)

57/63	Audience
0/69	Holy Spirit
60/63	Pardoner

---

62 Of avarice and . . .   400/114
The Pardoner now gives a carefully calculated summary of his technique, intention and attitude so that his audience will have no doubt in their minds as to what is happening. The constant repetition and amplification of the essential elements in the sermon were obviously important if the listening audience, as opposed to a reader, were to be kept aware of the preacher's intentions and follow his line of thought.

56/65	Rhetoric
47/65	Structure

---

63 Of avarice and . . .   400/114
You will recall the Latin tag 'radix . . . cupiditas'; here the Pardoner gives a clear account of what he means by 'cupiditas'. His only concern is with *his* avarice, in the guise of freeing his audience from *their* avarice. To what extent has the Pardoner so far demonstrated that the 'lewed' people are also avaricious, and in what way are they avaricious? Is there any distinction to be drawn between the avarice of the Pardoner and that of his audience? Are their motives the same?

61/69	Audience
58/72	Avarice
61/64	Pardoner

---

64 For myn entente . . .   403/117
If we did not already believe in the Pardoner's totally reprehensible nature, then his statement here that he is completely unconcerned about the 'correccioun of synne' ought to allay any doubts. His lack of concern for the eternal fate of his audiences' souls hits at the core of religious belief and it is a striking example of the man's utter cynicism and lack of conscience.

One of the prerequisites for the committing of mortal sin is encapsulated in the word 'entencioun'. Here and on a number of other occasions the

63/66	Pardoner
56/66	Sin

Pardoner uses the word, making clear his ready acknowledgement of being responsible for his own actions. It is also worth noting that he seems determined that his pilgrim audience shall be fully aware he has no care for any good that his sermons may by chance do.

He launches into his *Prologue* and *Tale* at the request of the Host, but is it already quite obvious that he has in mind to do more than just entertain his fellow pilgrims? An analysis of what you feel are his intentions and motives will be crucial to an understanding of both the Pardoner and his tale.

65 I rekke nevere . . .   405/119
The Pardoner spends time explaining some of the detail of how he goes about his preaching. He emphasizes his lack of concern for what happens to the soul, indicates how he indulges in slanderous comments, and refers, if we have not already noted it, to his venomous nature.

62/66	Rhetoric
62/72	Structure

Look at how his techniques and attitudes are reflected: honeyed words hide his venom; good sermons can stem from hate and hypocrisy; from evil intentions good can come. Again we have statement and restatement, the continuous repetition and amplification of his message so that his listening audience may more easily grasp and follow the significance of what is happening.

66 For certes, many a . . .   407/121
Given the Pardoner's dismissal a few moments ago of the fate of souls, would you consider that he is here making a feeble attempt at justifying his actions? It may well be that good sermons have issued from 'yvel entencioun' but does that excuse 'flaterye', 'ypocrisye', 'veyne glorie' or 'hate'? Or is he being totally 'world weary' and honest in his appraisal of sermonizing? Do remember that in the *Pardoner's Tale* and *Prologue* we are seeing the world through his eyes, and it can be very easy to take such statements as have just been given as being the only word on the subject.

64/69	Pardoner
65/70	Rhetoric
64/68	Sin

67 Comth ofte tyme of . . .   408/122
Is there a certain irony here in the Pardoner's contention that good can come of evil-intentioned sermons, when one considers the intent and possible effects of his sermons?

49/72	Irony

68 Som for plesance . . .   409/123
Would it be reasonable to include any of the following examples of 'yvel entencioun' amongst the 'seven deadly sins', and do any of them feature among the Pardoner's reasons for preaching?

66/69	Sin

69 Thanne wol I stynge . . .   413/127
The sin against the Holy Spirit which Christ mentioned (Matthew 12:31–32) is effectively claiming God's grace as springing from evil. Would you consider that there is a parallel here with the Pardoner's argument, just recently put, that there is many a good sermon that springs from evil intention?

63/70	Audience
60/112	Background
61/76	Holy Spirit
66/70	Pardoner
68/77	Sin

(You may recall the passage in the New Testament (Acts 2:4) when the Holy Spirit came upon the Apostles and they spoke with diverse tongues to the assembled peoples from various lands.) Most certainly the Pardoner uses his powers of speech to great effect, but in total abuse, we may assume, of God's purpose. Note how here and a little further on the Pardoner makes plain his own abuse of the power of speech and the evil intent to which he puts it. Would you consider that in using the pulpit to 'stynge' and 'defamed falsly' a man, he compounds his own offence? Note also that the latter is a sin against one of the Ten Commandments.

The medieval audience would no doubt be much more aware than we are of how the Pardoner is compounding sin upon sin in his description of how he goes about his work. Chaucer was concerned about the shame into which parts of the Church were falling and that concern shows through in this *Tale*, and others.

(In your reading you might like to consider to what extent Chaucer also shows the Pardoner as guilty of sinning against the three theological virtues, faith, hope and charity, in his attitude towards his audiences and the religious abuses he perpetrates upon them.)

---

70 For though I telle . . .   417/131

The Pardoner well knows how to broadcast the identity of someone whose character he wishes to defame, 'opening' men's eyes to the supposed evil; yet, as here, he seems to assume that he is able to lay bare his own mode of working to his audience and still believe he can work his will on them. It suggests a massive disregard for the intelligence of his listeners and an overweening regard for his own abilities – but is he right?

69/83	Audience
69/71	Pardoner
66/72	Rhetoric

---

71 Thus spitte I . . .   422/135

Note the tremendous contrast pointed at here between the Pardoner's attitude, 'spitte I out my venym' and the guise he uses for it, 'semen hooly and trewe'. It is well worth dwelling for a moment on the stark contrast contained in the imagery of 'spit' and 'venym' which is hidden by 'holiness' and 'truth'. Can you see here also the reflection hinted at of the sin against the Holy Spirit mentioned above in comment 69? The revelation says a lot about the character of the Pardoner.

70/72	Pardoner

---

72 I preche no thynge . . .   424/138

Yet again the Pardoner reiterates that his sole and overriding concern is with 'coveityse'.

If we haven't already gained sufficient insight into the Pardoner's motives and intentions, over the next few lines he provides an admirable summary for the reader. Here he confirms that the sole subject of his preaching is avarice. The irony of that statement will be highlighted at the end of this passage of ten lines.

63/75	Avarice
67/89	Irony
71/76	Pardoner
70/74	Rhetoric
65/73	Structure

---

73 I preche no thynge . . .   424/138

Again we have the idea restated that from evil, good may come. This is a very dangerous philosophy by which to attempt the justification of an evil action – but note that whilst the Pardoner states it may happen he does not try to capitalize on it to justify himself, rather he emphasizes to his audience that he cares not if good comes or does not come, only if profit comes to him.

72/79	Structure

---

74 Therfore my theme . . .   425/139

Again he repeats the Latin tag first met in line 334/48, and which he obviously seems to relish both for the irony it contains and the effect it presumably has on his audience. Note also the link it gives with the central

42/84	Language
72/81	Rhetoric

story in the actual *Tale*, the importance he attaches to this tag foreshadowing the theme later to be developed in detail.

---

75 Radix malorum est . . .   426/140
As he began his *Prologue*, so he continues. If his listeners did not understand its meaning earlier, they must surely understand now exactly what the Pardoner means by 'cupiditas'. Do you?

72/76   Avarice

---

76 Thus kan I . . .   427/141
The Pardoner recognizes his own vice, that of avarice. Do you consider that he is incapable of repenting, or would not repent, his sin and thus places himself in that category of sins against the Holy Spirit, obstinacy in sin? Here we see repeated the Pardoner briefly summarizing the great paradox of his practising the very thing he preaches against, but not simply that; for it is the very act of preaching against avarice that sees the Pardoner being his most avaricious self!

75/88   Avarice
69/127   Holy Spirit
72/77   Pardoner

---

77 But though myself . . .   429/143
You may recall the reference earlier to the sin of being wilful in one's acts against God. Here the Pardoner reemphasizes his knowledge and intent, going on to repeat the essence of his previous claim that through his own evil he can make others 'soore to repent'.

76/78   Pardoner
69/78   Sin

---

78 Yet kan I maken . . .   430/144
To what extent is this comment a sort of reversed echo of his contention that many a good sermon springs from evil intention? Could a good result spring from his evil intentions and actions?

77/79   Pardoner
77/86   Sin

---

79 But that is nat . . .   432/146
Having held out the small hope that good might come of his actions, the Pardoner reiterates his principal 'entente', and so rounds off this short summary with words that almost, but not quite, exactly reflect those that began it. Having informed us that he preaches only of avarice, he now concludes with the nicely ironic touch that he only preaches with avaricious intentions.

78/82   Pardoner
73/80   Structure

---

80 Of this mateere . . .   434/148
One perhaps cannot be blamed for agreeing with the sentiments expressed here by the Pardoner. But can the Pardoner ever say enough about avarice, of which he is the very embodiment? It would seem the answer is no. For in the next few lines we shall see how he yet again plumbs the depths to which he is prepared to sink in order to gain a secure and comfortable living and future for himself.

79/81   Structure

Is the Pardoner perhaps so struck by the monstrousness of his own behaviour that he is experimenting on his audience to see what their reaction to his revelations is? Would he enjoy a horrified reaction, and is that what he gets from the Host at the end of the tale?

The problem of why the Pardoner opens his 'heart' to the audience is only partly answered by referring to our experiences of the stock stage villain who throughout history has revealed himself in all his villainy by speaking directly to his audience. With the Pardoner we have much more of a conundrum and no obviously 'correct' answers. You might like to consider whether the Pardoner is beyond redemption, or indeed if he wishes for redemption. Is it possible that someone can preach so effectively against a sin and yet fall so fully into it? Or is what we are seeing a measure of how effectively evil ensnares one, just as will be exemplified in the tale to be told by the Pardoner of the three rioters?

81 Thanne telle I . . .   435/149

The Pardoner is now leading up to the actual *Tale* itself and puts the final piece of his sermonizing technique into place, explaining that he uses old and popular stories to illustrate his sermons and drive his message home. In doing so he shows again his knowledge of how best to reach his audience's purse. Can you see how at the same time he shows his contempt for the very people who effectively give him his living?

74/92	Rhetoric
80/82	Structure

82 What, trowe ye . . .   439/153

Here we are given an insight into what the Pardoner hopes to get out of his activities: his intent to have a full belly, warmth and a 'wenche in evry toun' proclaims his own self-interest above all. He exclaims against the notion that he would willingly live in poverty when he can earn so much by preaching. What is the greater sin in his eyes, to live in poverty or to live well by causing others poverty? The latter he is well prepared to do, as will now be seen.

79/83	Pardoner
81/91	Structure

83 Nay, nay, I thoghte . . .   442/156

Do you think his audience really needed this confirmation of the Pardoner's intentions? To what extent, if at all, do you feel that this exclamatory reassurance is put there in an attempt to raise a laugh from his audience and to an extent lessen the force of his previous disclosures?

70/92	Audience
82/84	Pardoner

84 For I wol preche . . .   443/157

Note the emphasis given by the repetition of the word 'wol' in this and other lines of this section. How do you think it helps to emphasize that the Pardoner is fully determined in his course of action?

74/109	Language
83/85	Pardoner

85 I wol nat do . . .   444/158

How is his determination to do no physical labour yet another passing, and by implication derogatory, reference to the 'lewed' people who provide him with his living?

84/86	Pardoner

86 I wol noon of . . .   447/161

You will be familiar with the modern meaning of counterfeit and its implication here is not so far removed. The Apostles were given a mission by Christ to spread His Gospel by preaching and example. When the Pardoner stands in a pulpit he pretends to be about 'Cristes hooly werk' and preaches against the evils of avarice: he adopts the externals of an Apostle's mission but every last piece of him is counterfeit.

18/167	Church
85/87	Pardoner
78/88	Sin

87 I wol have moneie . . .   448/162

Note how the Pardoner is prepared to take anything he can in 'payment' for his services. The 'wolle, chese and whete' makes it plain whom he is exploiting.

86/88	Pardoner

88 Al sholde hir children . . .   451/165
It is perhaps fitting that a threat to the most precious possession common to poor people throughout the world, their children, should draw the Pardoner's catalogue of avaricious intent to a close, as he tells how he would willingly visit famine upon them.

76/95	Avarice
87/89	Pardoner
86/90	Sin

89 Nay, I wol drynke . . .   452/166
One can perhaps imagine the Pardoner flourishing his drink as he says this line. You will remember that the pilgrims have stopped for a while at a tavern. What might be the effect on the audience of his concern with his own belly, so immediately after speaking of children dying of starvation?

25/93	Drunkenness
88/90	Pardoner
72/92	Irony

90 And have a joly . . .   453/167
Reference has previously been made to the uncertain nature of the Pardoner's masculinity and to seeming contradictions between the description of him in the introduction contained in the *General Prologue* to *The Canterbury Tales*, and how he describes himself and his actions in his own *Prologue*. Do we now have another contradiction? Certainly for a man as avaricious as the Pardoner, gross sexual appetite would be nothing strange, but is it in character? Might you want to distinguish between lecherous talk and deeds? There is so much about the man that is a sham, that this might be but one more example.

| 89/93 | Pardoner |
| 88/97 | Sin |

91 But herkneth, lordynges . . .   454/168
The final section of the *Prologue* reminds the Pardoner's audience that he is in a tavern, drinking. This is an important reminder as it foreshadows not only the initial setting for the tale he is about to tell, but also epitomizes the sources of satisfaction for himself and the three rioters about whom we shall shortly hear: drunkenness, blasphemy, gluttony and lechery.

The Pardoner, if the audience is in any doubt, sums up his own character – a 'ful vicious man' – but yet again points up the seeming contradiction, 'A moral tale yet I yow telle kan'.

| 82/92 | Structure |

92 But herkneth, lordynges . . .   454/168
You should note the ways in which Chaucer achieves balance and continuity between the various sections of the *Prologue* and *Tale*, and also in relation to the Pardoner's introduction in the *General Prologue*. This reference to 'lordynges', a repetition of his mode of address to them at the beginning of his *Prologue*, is but a small example of such techniques. The balance is not just stylistically but is most obvious in the way that the introduction in the *General Prologue*, the *Prologue* and *Tale* are built one from another, with theme, and character delineation of the Pardoner, introduced, exemplified and developed. Is there an ironic touch in his use of the word 'lordynges', a gentle mocking of his audience? If they are 'gentil' then they must surely have been scandalized by the Pardoner's address so far.

83/134	Audience
89/94	Irony
81/115	Rhetoric
91/93	Structure

93 Now have I dronke . . .   456/170
It is perhaps appropriate that he should draw attention to the fact that he has finished his draft of 'corny ale' before beginning his *Tale*. His *Tale* is full of drunken riot, and indeed, the three rioters drink their fill before embarking on their search for Death.

89/96	Drunkenness
90/94	Pardoner
92/103	Structure

94 For though myself . . . 459/173

Yet again the Pardoner refers to the irony contained in the idea of a 'ful vicious man' preaching a 'moral tale'. How far would you judge him to be fully responsible for his actions?

To what extent do we now know the character of the Pardoner? Is he actually someone to whom we can relate as a believable person, or has he become too much of a stereotype in this *Prologue* which has dwelt in so much detail on the almost limitless extent of his sinful character? Consider whether he is just the personification of man's rejection of God, a symbol himself, much like the nameless rioters of his tale.

95 Which I am wont . . . 461/175

This, then, is the sermon about which he has spoken so much in the *Prologue*. It is perhaps appropriate that he has learnt it off by heart as it brings to him the thing that is closest to his heart, money.

The Pardoner's Tale

96 In Flaunders whilom . . . 463/177

You will recall that the pilgrims have stopped at a tavern whilst the Pardoner has a drink. It is perhaps appropriate that the sermon should be set in a particular region, the Low Countries, which in those days was popularly associated with heavy drinking.

97 As riot, hasard . . . 465/179

What follows is a list of all the vices that these young people engage in. You will note that even from the outset of their description, like the depths of his own character which the Pardoner has recently revealed to us, these three rioters are seen to be already probably beyond redemption. In particular the Pardoner here comments on their debauchery and lechery, in the 'stewes' or brothels of the area. Why might such activities be close to the Pardoner's heart? It is worth noting here that in contrast to the Pardoner, the rioters are not fully developed as characters. Their relatively brief appearance as they hasten recklessly to their death allows no such possibility.

98 And eten also and . . . 468/182

The drunkenness and gluttony which were mentioned in the *Prologue* are quickly reiterated and attributed to the rioters as well. The Pardoner's comment that the tavern is the 'develes temple' echoes the medieval view of the happenings that occur in such places. It increases the irony, then, that he should, before telling his tale, have insisted on quenching his thirst in a tavern.

99 By superfluytee abhomynable . . . 471/185

Why might you consider that both the Pardoner and the rioters are but personifications of the sins they exemplify?

100 Hir othes been so . . .   472/186
Note the speed with which the Pardoner moves through the whole gamut of sins the rioters commit. Such speed is also reflected in the swiftness with which they make up their minds to do things and with which they carry them out. They are here in marked contrast to the Pardoner who quite obviously calculates carefully exactly where and when his best interests lie. The *Tale* moves swiftly from the excesses of the body to comment on the blasphemous speech of the rioters.

94/102 Pardoner
99/148 Rioters
97/101 Sin

101 Oure blissed Lordes . . .   474/188
This swearing by Christ's body is a nice contrast to the 'devel sacrifise' just previously mentioned. Do you think that the Pardoner is, in effect, equally guilty of the crime implied here when he says he is about 'Cristes holy werk'?

100/102 Sin

102 To kyndle and blowe . . .   481/195
Can you see echoes here first of the introduction to the Pardoner in the *General Prologue*, and then of the Pardoner in his own *Prologue*? Note how the three are linked, with one building upon and amplifying with great detail previously mentioned matters. This process of amplification will shortly be continued when the Pardoner begins his digression about sin, before returning to the matter of the rioters and their tale.

100/104 Pardoner
101/104 Sin

103 The hooly writ . . .   483/197
The Pardoner is now about to move from the specific sins of this 'compaignye' to a much wider consideration of those sins just mentioned, and in a context which enables him to show off his knowledge of the Bible and such matters of history as he feels are useful to him.

You might like to look back over the sins just mentioned and consider the irony of the Pardoner preaching against them. How many of them has he demonstrated to us as being special to himself?

93/108 Structure

104 That luxurie is . . .   484/198
The medieval audience would have been familiar with the many sins which have so far been flourished in front of them. They would also have known the Biblical view about what the wages of sin were. Is the irony here that the rioters, for all their supposed worldliness, cannot see what it is they are rushing headlong into, and the Pardoner is equally fooled by his own rhetoric and sinful nature?

98/110 Irony
102/105 Pardoner
102/110 Sin

105 Lo, how that dronken . . .   485/199
Neatly linking two of his sins, drunkenness and lechery, with incest, the Pardoner refers to the Old Testament story of Lot. Note how Lot was so drunk it took away any knowledge of what he was doing. To that extent then, would you consider there was a mitigating feature to his actions but not to the origin of those actions, drunkenness?

Can the Pardoner claim any such mitigating circumstances for his excesses in sin?

50/106 Bible
98/106 Drunkenness
104/111 Pardoner

106 Herodes, whoso wel . . .   488/202
It is doubtful that the 'lewed' people would have knowledge of the detail of

105/110 Bible

Biblical stories. They were not to know that there was no evidence at all of   105/107   Drunkenness
Herod being drunk with wine when he called for John the Baptist's head. He
may have been drunk with lust for Salome, but again there is no evidence to
support that. However, the Pardoner's use of this 'story' to support the
point he is making is quite effective.

---

107 He seith he kan . . .   493/207
The distinction drawn by Seneca, a philosopher who lived (?)4BC–65AD, is   106/125   Drunkenness
a matter of degree. Having given two examples of the madness brought on
by drink the Pardoner suggests that the only redeeming feature of
drunkenness is that, unlike madness, at least it comes to an end.

---

108 O glotonye, ful . . .   498/212
Note how a very similar series of declamations followed by a reference to   103/122   Structure
Christ in the fourth line is also to be found just after the Pardoner tells us of
the murders committed by the three rioters. Are there any similarities
between the situations he describes in these two parts and in the Pardoner's
intentions?

---

109 O glotonye, ful . . .   498/212
Having given two brief examples and drawn a not very comforting parallel,   98/113   Gluttony
the Pardoner now launches into a series of exclamatory lines which build   84/120   Language
into a climax and lead us into the next section of his digression before the
Tale proper. Gluttony is a sin that encompasses drunkenness, lechery, and
many others; would you consider avarice to be a sin covered by gluttony?

One can perhaps imagine this sudden declamation of the Pardoner allowing
him to raise his voice and bring any wandering minds in his audience back
under his spell. Certainly the images compressed within three lines:
'glotonye, cursednesse, confusioun, dampnacioun', and the repeated 'O, O,
O' which precedes them, has a dramatic effect.

---

110 O cause first of . . .   499/214
This reference to the first cause of our confusion takes us back to the story of   106/114   Bible
Adam and Eve. You might like to consider the irony of the Pardoner's   104/113   Irony
reference to Adam, who is also known as the 'man without regenerating   104/131   Sin
grace'. Well might such a description apply to the Pardoner.

Would you consider that this reference to Adam and Eve provides a link to
the snake image suggested by 'spitte I out my venym', and to the Pardoner's
obvious penchant for the attractions of a pretty woman? You may recall that
Eve was tempted by the serpent and subsequently herself tempted Adam.
Consider also the implications contained in the picture which often shows
the Virgin Mary as standing on and crushing a serpent, and the obvious
contrast she is to the objects of the Pardoner's and the rioters' lecherous
thoughts and deeds.

Given the major part played by religion in the lives of medieval man, they
would have seen far more clearly than we do the many associated ideas
which are contained in much of what the Pardoner says and does.

---

111 O original of oure . . .   500/215
Would you consider that the Pardoner actually includes himself amongst   105/112   Pardoner
those who are damned?

---

112 Til Crist hadde boght . . .   501/215

There was a controversy in the Middle Ages which concerned the matter of the Eucharistic Feast and Chaucer's audience would most likely have been aware of it – certainly Chaucer himself would have been. Is this the first reference to Christ's body and the sacrifice He made?

The belief then current (and which for many still prevails) was that in the Eucharist, the bread and wine actually became Christ's body and blood; but it was a belief that was starting to be questioned. The Pardoner will make a clearer reference to the question later in this section.

113 Corrupt was al this . . .   504/218

How ironic do you consider these words of the Pardoner to be, given his own attitude to sin as evidenced so far in his *Prologue* and *Tale*?

114 Adam, oure fader . . .   505/219

Not the first Biblical reference, and like so many other examples he gives, the Pardoner is not strictly accurate in his description of the reason for Adam's and Eve's dismissal from the Garden of Eden.

Whatever the reason for their fall, the Pardoner is now leading up to a whole section which concentrates on the evils to be derived from gluttony. It suits his purpose to use the story of man's catastrophic fall from grace as a preamble to his own sermon on the horrendous dangers to man's soul of the sin of gluttony.

115 Allas! the shorte . . .   517/231

Chaucer's audience would be more familiar with the many quotations that the Pardoner 'lifts' from the New Testament and other sources. The resounding phrases serve his rhetoric well.

116 Of this matiere . . .   521/235

The reference to St Paul's discourse again stretches the imagination to see how it covers gluttony, but the accuracy of the Pardoner's Biblical or other references is not really the important aspect here. What is important is his technique in appealing to a source which his listeners are not in a position to query. Equally, his seeming familiarity with Biblical and other erudite references reinforces his own status and by inference, that of his pardons and rag-bag of relics.

There is not much about the Pardoner which we could call honest; his relics and pardons are forgeries, and even his Bible stories and historical references are manipulated and changed to suit the purposes of his sermon.

117 That of his throte . . .   527/241

From 'tendre mouth' a few lines before, the Pardoner brings his listeners up with a jolt as he introduces the deliberately coarse idea of the mouth becoming a toilet. You may notice that his technique of revealing more and damaging revelations about himself in the *Prologue*, finds a parallel here, as he now proceeds to develop this particular image in a far more revolting way than perhaps the subject demands.

What is it in the Pardoner's character that fuels the need to confront and shock his audience? He does it when he painstakingly reveals his own 'ful vicious' character. He is doing it now in this preamble to the tale of the three rioters.

---

118 The apostle wepyng . . .   529/243

Using all his skills, the Pardoner now presents an image of the apostle 'wepying . . . pitously'. From a toilet image we move swiftly to the picture of a weeping, distraught apostle, and then, as swiftly, on to an image calculated to induce even greater reaction from his enthralled (or horrified) audience.

117/119   Rhetoric

---

119 Of whiche the ende . . .   533/247

What is it do you think that is the Pardoner's god? We know that he gains great wealth from his work, but do you think that he perhaps gains almost as great a reward from the very act of preaching; by enthralling and holding his audience with words and glorying in the power he feels he has over them? Would you consider that power is evidenced by the very success of his preaching in that his audience *do* fill his pockets with money?

117/124   Pardoner
118/120   Rhetoric

---

120 O wombe! O bely! . . .   534/248

This is another declamation which mirrors the previous one, but here he compresses his ideas into one line.

Previously he took his audience back to the Biblical origins of man, now he centres the image on man's belly and enlarges on the corruption in it and that issues from it. You might like to ponder, in comparison, how 'foul is the soun' that issues from the Pardoner in the form of his sermon (not the surface form but the twisted spirit within). Note the tremendous contrast with the foregoing lofty image of the Apostle weeping and the down-to-earth 'stynkyng cod' and 'dong'.

It is very easy to get caught up in the effectiveness of his rhetoric and allow to slip from our minds his declared purpose in so preaching. Have you, and has his pilgrim audience by now forgotten the 'children sterve for famyne' and that by his own words he is a 'ful vicious man' who cares not for the fate of souls?

114/127   Gluttony
109/122   Language
119/125   Rhetoric

---

121 And turnen substaunce . . .   539/253

This is a more pointed reference to the growing controversy over the interpretation of Christ's words when he instituted the Eucharist. The Eucharist is the central part of the Mass and can only be celebrated by a duly and properly ordained priest.

The Pardoner previously introduced imagery relating to cooking in his prologue when he referred to his preaching techniques and the use of Latin. The Mass was celebrated in Latin and perhaps here we see the fulfilment of the cooking image.

Are the cooks an image for the priests who take bread and wine to transform them into Christ's body and blood whilst it still retains the appearance of bread and wine? Certainly the use of such technical words as 'substaunce' and 'accident' which relate directly to this controversy suggests that perhaps the Pardoner is here being quite outrageously provocative and blasphemous in the way he is associating ideas and images of the body, dung, corruption, and Christ.

112/130   Background

122 That may go thurgh . . .   543/257
Notice the contrast here between the 'stampe', 'streyne', 'grynde' of a few
lines back as the cooks prepare their 'corruptions' for the belly, and,
contrastingly, the sensuous sounding 'softe' and 'swoote' as they pass
through the 'golet', picking up and to an extent rounding off the image
contained in 'tendre mouth' in line 517.

120/126	Language
108/123	Structure

---

123 Shal been his sauce . . .   545/259
There is not a world of difference between 'saffron' and 'sauce', certainly
not where the Pardoner is concerned. Look at the associations in the next
four lines between the detail he gives to the pilgrims in his *Prologue* of how
he goes about his sermons and the comments he makes here.

122/125	Structure

---

124 Is deed, whil that . . .   548/262
How accurate a description would you consider this to be of the Pardoner:
'dead though living in his vices'?

119/128	Pardoner

---

125 A lecherous thyng . . .   549/263
Combining two images, drunkenness and lechery, the Pardoner now
concentrates his attention on the evils of drink.

Notice how the solemn declamatory tone of the previous lines now changes
as the Pardoner injects an element of levity, if not actual humour, into his
sermon. However, running true to form he maintains the sense of the
grotesque.

107/128	Drunkenness
120/133	Rhetoric
123/134	Structure

---

126 A lecherous thyng . . .   549/263
Note how wine and drunkenness are personified, 'lecherous . . . stryvyng
. . . wrecchednesse' and as they are disfigured so is the man who drinks the
wine and becomes drunk.

122/127	Language

---

127 And thurgh thy . . .   553/267
The 'soun' of drunkenness becomes a slightly amusing reference to the
onomatopoeic qualities of snoring and the Biblical character Samson. Note
the link which is made here with the preceding part of the declamation
which also spent some little time on the 'soun' which issued at both ends of
the gluttonous body!

The Pardoner's sermon concentrates on the sinful excesses that can ensue
from such gluttony, but does his sin, perhaps the greatest of all sins (against
the Holy Spirit) issue through the mouth, not from a corrupt belly, but from
a diseased soul?

120/139	Gluttony
76/225	Holy Spirit
126/160	Language

---

128 Thy tonge is lost . . .   557/271
How close to the Pardoner's heart would be this concern that the 'tonge is
lost' as is 'mannes wit and his discrecioun' through drunkenness? Would it
be fair to say that the Pardoner, in his *Prologue* to the *Tale* 'lost' his tongue
and showed very little wit and even less discretion in the manner through
which he revealed himself and his practices to his fellow pilgrims? Was he
'drunk' with self-confidence and vainglory?

125/132	Drunkenness
113/145	Irony
124/129	Pardoner

129 He kan no conseil . . .   561/275
Is this an accurate description of the Pardoner, as well as the drunkard?

---

130 And namely fro . . .   563/277
There is a reference here to the practice of watering down good wines with cheaper varieties. The audience would have understood these references and perhaps enjoyed the digs being made. Chaucer, as a vintner's son would have had firsthand knowledge of any such malpractices.

---

131 Thurgh verray God . . .   576/290
The Pardoner is saying that all of those great things recorded in the Old Testament were achieved only through abstinence and prayer and then only by the grace of God, who, being omnipotent, sees and knows all things.

Do you think the Pardoner believes what he says here? If he does believe in an omnipotent God then his (the Pardoner's) every action and word is an outright and knowing rejection of God. He is on record as caring nothing for the souls of those he cheats, so what do you feel is his belief about his own soul and its long-term fate, if he thinks that far ahead?

How crucial would you consider this point to be for an understanding of what Chaucer is saying about the Pardoner and the extent to which his audience would understand the nature of the Pardoner's sin?

When you read of the three rioters' headlong dash towards the pile of gold and death, you might like to consider whether their avarice is paralleled by that of the Pardoner, and that perhaps one of the main differences between them is that he proceeds on his flight to death for the same avaricious reasons but at a much more leisurely and considered pace!

---

132 Looke, Attila, the . . .   579/293
Among the final images in this section on gluttony is a reference to Attila bleeding through his nose in a drunken sleep. Is this the first reference to drunkenness causing death? Was the Pardoner being ironic in his reference to Attila being the 'grete conquerour'? There's not much greatness contained in the picture of a 'great' man drunk, and bleeding to death through his nose.

---

133 Nat Samuel, but . . .   585/299
It is again typical that the Pardoner should indulge in a little display of learning, hastening to assure his audience that he knows the difference between Samuel and Lamuel. Quite obviously he would be aware that his audience would not have been looking to see if he made a mistake in his references.

---

134 And now that I . . .   589/303
The Pardoner now 'steps outside' the text of his sermon to speak directly to his audience and in so doing marks another stage in its structure. He has completed his major consideration of gluttony, and will now move on to consider the sin of gambling.

---

135 And now that I . . .   589/303
To what extent do you feel that this announcement of the new topic not only

marks the careful structure of his sermonizing technique, but also that he is quite aware of what he is doing and the effect he wants to achieve in relation to the pilgrims who are listening to him?

133/139	Rhetoric
134/140	Structure

136 Hasard is verray . . .   591/305
The Pardoner suggests that gambling is the mother of lies, deceit, forswearing (perjury), blasphemy and manslaughter, as well as a waste of time and goods. Would you consider that manslaughter is a curious inclusion in this list and can you think why it should be mentioned here?

0/137	Gambling

137 Hasard is verray . . .   591/305
In the following list of 'lesynges', or lies, to what extent do you consider them to be very much sins that we could also attribute to the Pardoner, especially in that the intention of his every word is to deceive?

136/139	Gambling
135/142	Pardoner

138 Blaspheme of Crist . . .   593/307
Note how the Pardoner here links the sin of 'blaspheme' with 'man-slaughtre'. The juxtaposition of these two ideas will now occur more frequently. We are seeing a clearer reference to the effect of the sin which is central to the Pardoner's activities.

131/144	Sin

139 It is repreeve and . . .   595/309
Picking up the reference a few lines back to the shame and dishonour of Attila, the Pardoner now suggests that gambling can also bring dishonour.

Note he also uses the start of his consideration of gambling to provide a general introduction to the evils which stem from it, prior to going into more detail.

137/140	Gambling
127/0	Gluttony
135/140	Rhetoric

140 And ever the hyer . . .   597/311
The Pardoner completes this section by concentrating on the view that the higher a man is in status, the greater will be his fall. In subsequent lines he will amplify this point by reference to historical examples, thus following the previous pattern when referring to gambling, and ensuring that his audience are clear as to the central point of this part of his sermon.

139/151	Gambling
139/141	Rhetoric
135/143	Structure

141 Stilboun, that was a . . .   603/317
One can perhaps imagine the Pardoner rolling these references to Stilboun, Corynthe and Lacedomye, Demetrius and Parthes off his tongue as he moves into the final section of his sermon before the example of the tale of the three rioters.

140/143	Rhetoric

142 And seyde, 'Ther wol . . .'   611/325
There is great play here on honour and name and the way in which it reflects the status and dignity of the person involved. The Pardoner makes clear that Stilboun is no 'whitened sepulchre', that is, a decorated and whitened receptacle for the dead which hides the corruption within.

Is there an implied comparison here with the character of the Pardoner?

137/147	Pardoner

143 Sente him a paire . . .   623/337
Where else do we see a reference to dice, but ones made of bone, not gold? You should note the constant repetition of imagery during the course of the *Pardoner's Prologue* and *Tale,* and the effect it has of giving continuity to the narrative, providing links to both structure and content.

141/146   Rhetoric
140/144   Structure

144 Now wol I speke . . .   629/343
It is no accident that the sin of blasphemy was left to the last, it is after all a direct assault on God's name and in direct contravention of the Commandments. One of the more obvious characteristics of the three rioters whose tale proper is about to begin, is the extent to which they blaspheme. Can you say to what extent and when, the Pardoner has been guilty of similar blasphemies?

22/145   Blasphemy
138/153   Sin
143/150   Structure

145 The heighe God . . .   633/347
There is an inherent irony in the Pardoner quoting Christ's own condemnation of blasphemy, when he himself indulges in it so frequently and apparently without advertance to Christ's own words.

143/147   Blasphemy
128/170   Irony

146 Witnesse on Mathew . . .   634/348
Again the Pardoner uses Biblical references to 'saffron' his sermon. Note that the pattern of references started with the Bible, moved on to classical events, and now finishes with a return to the Bible: Matthew, Jeremiah, and, shortly, the Ten Commandments.

143/152   Rhetoric

147 'Take nat my name . . .'   642/356
To what extent do you feel the Pardoner indulges in such a course as is described here?

144/148   Blasphemy
142/152   Pardoner

148 By Goddes precious herte . . .   651/365
When considering the matter of blasphemy, you ought to bear in mind, yet again, the central importance of the Church in the lives of medieval man. Note how the examples he gives here will find their fulfilment in the mouths of the three rioters.

147/151   Blasphemy
100/149   Rioters

149 By Goddes armes, if . . .   654/368
This reference to 'falsly pleye' will find its reflection in the activities of the rioters, who will indeed play false with each other, with one of them suffering from a dagger.

148/158   Rioters

150 This fruyt cometh . . .   656/370
The reference to dice and bones nicely picks up and contrasts with the previous reference to golden dice, and perhaps also puts us in mind of the pigs' bones which the Pardoner carries around with him.

144/151   Structure

151 Forsweryng, ire, falsnesse . . .   675/371
Note how these references are reminiscent of a list from the beginning of this section on blasphemy. It also effectively refers us to the beginning of the discourse on gambling when a similar list was also presented. Would you consider that the 'manslaughtre' mentioned then in almost the same breath

148/172   Blasphemy
140/0   Gambling
150/153   Structure

as 'blaspheme of Crist' finds its reflection and extension in this reference to
the more serious sin of 'homycide'?

152 Now for the love . . .   658/372

The Pardoner would seem to be demonstrating his total lack of sincerity, for
in calling on the love of God he indulges in the very sin that he has just so
eloquently condemned.

To what extent is Chaucer again drawing our attention to the crucial nature
of the Pardoner's sin, in it being knowingly and without any shame a
rejection of God's love and grace?

147/180	Pardoner
146/170	Rhetoric

153 Now for the love . . .   658/372

Note how we are now brought back to the central theme of the *Pardoner's
Tale*, the rejection of God's love through sin.

144/220	Sin
151/154	Structure

154 But, sires, now . . .   660/374

After a long digression the Pardoner again speaks directly to his audience to
mark the end of that part of his sermon which considered the nature of the
sins of gluttony, gambling and blasphemy. Now he turns to a tale which will
concern 'real' people who exemplify those sins and their consequences. The
word digression perhaps suggests that the Pardoner 'wandered off' his
subject a little – do you think he did?

153/155	Structure

155 Thise riotoures thre . . .   661/375

The return to his tale proper marks the beginning of the climax to the
Pardoner's whole performance.

The rioters have been drinking long before the beginning of prayers at the
start of daylight and the bell that marks them. Note the reference to the bell
in association with prayers at the start of a new day. This will very shortly be
replaced by a reference to the bell rung at the procession of a corpse, one
which will not bode well for the rioters.

0/157	Death
154/162	Structure

156 Were set hem in . . .   663/377

As we left the Pardoner drinking at a tavern, so we meet the rioters sitting in
a tavern, already very drunk if we are to take account of the length of time
they have been there.

132/163	Drunkenness

157 Biforn a cors . . .   665/379

Already in the tale we have encountered drunkenness; now this is followed
quickly by an image of death. Life expectancy in the Middle Ages was very
short, and death was a constant companion to the whole population. Also,
they were not inured to the fact of death as we are in the 20th century:
dealing with the dead, however close a relative they may be, is almost
always someone else's job.

You must also take account of the fact that it was in the 14th century that the
Black Death on three occasions swept through England and killed around
one third of the population. In some places entire communities were wiped
out, as we shall shortly hear.

130/165	Background
155/158	Death

158 That oon of hem . . .   666/380

So far no names have been given to any of the three rioters, and now when one of them calls to his 'knave', also lacking a name, he asks particularly for the name of the dead person. Despite this request however, he will not be obliged.

So far in the *Tale* and *Prologue* the only names used have been those of long dead Biblical or classical characters. The only 'name' we have is that of Pardoner, whose name but exemplifies his profession, and whose profession is his name. The only 'real' character that possesses a name, as we shall shortly see, is Death, whom the rioters and the Old Man both seek.

If Death is the only reality in the story, it is a reality which neither the Pardoner nor the three rioters seem ever to actually conceive as something which will overcome them. It is considered by the former as a frightening concept to be used as a means to persuade others to repent and purchase worthless relics and pardons, and by the latter as something to be sought out and 'killed'.

157/162	Death
149/159	Rioters

159 'Go bet,' quod he . . .   667/381

This injunction to the boy to hasten on the quest for the dead man's name foreshadows the almost indecent haste with which they pursue their headlong rush to their own deaths. Their concern to know the name will be answered, in a way, by the boy's response – can you see how?

0/161	Haste
158/161	Rioters

160 'Sire,' quod this boy . . .   670/384

Note the character of this boy and his message. It is straightforward good sense and advice – which seems older than his 'years'. Be aware of the short, simple sentence construction in marked contrast to much of the Pardoner's sermon. How does it compare with the speech of the rioters and the Old Man?

0/161	Boy
127/161	Language

161 'Sire,' quod this boy . . .   670/384

Note the polite address of the boy, which will be quite the reverse of the speech of the rioters. The foreknowledge the boy displays prevents any delay in the bad news being given to his questioner. The boy has known who it was for two hours, and declining to name the person perhaps ominously imparts the knowledge that it was a former companion of the rioters.

160/168	Boy
159/178	Haste
160/167	Language
159/162	Rioters

162 He was, pardee . . .   672/386

Do you find it appropriate that the first death should be a companion of the rioters? Note how it anticipates the death of the rioters who also will be 'sodeynly . . . yslayn'.

158/163	Death
161/166	Rioters
155/167	Structure

163 Fordronke, as he sat . . .   674/388

The Pardoner's declamation on the dangers of drunkenness finds a partial fulfilment here in this description of the former companion of the rioters, slain in a drunken sleep.

162/164	Death
156/0	Drunkenness

164 Ther cam a privee . . .   675/389

Note the personification of Death as a thief who comes in the night. This in

163/165	Death

itself is rather ominous for the rioters. They will have difficulty enough in trying to identify him.

---

165 He hath a thousand . . .   679/393

As previously mentioned the Black Death three times swept through England. The death and pestilence which followed in its train had left an indelible mark on the century. In one sense, the later determination of the rioters to seek out and slay Death can be understood, but equally it flies in the face of the common experience of men.

The fact that Death should have slain so many, and yet still the rioters wish to seek him out, gives us yet another perspective from which to view the depths of sin into which they have fallen. It is sin which prevents them from a recognition of their own folly and culpability.

157/0	Background
164/166	Death

---

166 And, maistre, er ye . . .   680/394

The solemn warning given here by the boy would remind his listeners of man's duty to prepare for death by repenting of one's sins and living a good life. The drunken state which it is probably fair to assume the three rioters are in, is hardly a fit condition in which to prepare an assault on Death. Does it also speak of their lack of spiritual preparation which will make them unfit to meet the fate they are most assuredly going to face?

165/169	Death
162/172	Rioters

---

167 Thus taughte me my . . .   684/398

There are two aspects to consider in this line with particular reference to 'taughte me my dame'.

Does the 'dame' pick up previous references to the Virgin Mary and the Pardoner's lechery, and, with the boy's obvious respect for his mother, provide a contrasting attitude?

Equally it might be that Chaucer's audience would see this as a reference to Holy Mother Church, a common enough image at the time.

Do also note how this image is picked up later on by the old man.

86/173	Church
161/168	Language
162/169	Structure

---

168 Thus taughte me my . . .   684/398

After this short appearance the boy has no more part to play. His final words, 'I sey namoore' are literally true, but what he has said ought to strike warning bells both for the rioters and the audience. Note the solemnity of his final words, almost as through he 'rests his case'. Would you agree that perhaps there is a tone of regret or failure in his words, as though he realized they were falling on deaf ears?

161/187	Boy
167/182	Language

---

169 'By seinte Marie!' . . .   685/399

This short speech by the taverner confirms the boy's words and adds the fateful information that he thinks he knows where Death lives. Note again the reference to 'seinte Marie'.

166/170	Death
167/203	Structure

---

170 To been avysed . . .   690/404

The taverner repeats the boy's advice, but note the irony of his comment about Death doing a man dishonour. Have the rioters any fear in this respect?

169/171	Death
145/171	Irony
152/181	Rhetoric

You will recall the comments about honour which occurred in the section on gambling and which were followed by a consideration of swearing. Here, the taverner's talk of honour is immediately followed by the rioter swearing by 'goddes armes'.

---

171 'Is it swich peril . . .'   693/407

It is ironic that the rioter is unable to see the peril in meeting Death. Having no ears for the boy's or the taverner's words of warning he proceeds immediately to seek out Death. In his drunken state he well exemplifies the Pardoner's warnings as to the fate drunkards will meet.

170/175   Death
170/173   Irony

---

172 I make avow to . . .   695/409

Yet again we have a reference to bones, but this time to God's bones. Note the violence of the rioter's language. The final examples given by the Pardoner were on the subject of swearing, and this man's constant blasphemies bring to our minds the words 'Forsweryng, ire, falsnesse, homycide'. To what extent are these all represented in this section?

151/176   Blasphemy
166/174   Rioters

---

173 Herkneth, felawes . . .   696/410

The irony of the rioters swearing to be as one will not be lost on the audience when the rioters turn on one another in their murderous avarice. What will be equally apparent to them is a blasphemous echo which speaks of a central doctrine of the Church, the Holy Trinity – 'we thre been al ones'.

167/187
171/177

---

174 And ech of us . . .   698/412

The mockery here in 'bicomen otheres brother' will become obvious as the *Tale* develops. Its mockery of the Commandments would be obvious to Chaucer's audience.

Before the *Tale* has almost got properly underway, our rioters have with undignified haste rushed into the very blasphemies the Pardoner warned of.

172/183   Rioters

---

175 And we wol sleen . . .   699/413

The intemperate reference to Death being a 'false traytour' perhaps ought to suggest that the rioters are the last people who ought to attempt a joust with Death. Certainly, 'traytour' is a word with some significance, especially bearing in mind the oath the rioters are to take to each other.

171/186   Death

---

176 By Goddes dignitee . . .   701/415

The final blasphemous oath in this section brings it to a fitting end. With the violence of their oaths and attitudes, can we be in any doubt as to the character of these men and their probable fate?

172/179   Blasphemy

---

177 To lyve and dyen . . .   703/417

No doubt the irony of these words will not be lost on the audience later in the *Tale*. The value of their oaths to each other may perhaps be judged by the state they are in 'dronken in this rage', and yet again the Pardoner brings back to his audience's mind one of the sins he is so eloquently preaching against.

173/180   Irony

178 And forth they . . .   706/420
Without the thought which both boy and taverner counselled them to use, the rioters hasten off on their quest for Death.

161/181   Haste

179 And Cristes blessed body . . .   709/423
You will recall the previous references to manslaughter and homicide which were followed closely by references to Christ. Do these now find their fulfilment in this image of Christ's body being rent by 'many a grisly ooth' which they swear?

176/180   Blasphemy

180 Deeth shal be deed . . .   710/424
The irony is that Christ died on His cross and overcame death. His sacrifice would seem to have been in vain for the three rioters, for they insist on crucifying him again with their constant blasphemy!

It is worth pausing a while to consider the contradiction contained in their quest – to bring death to Death. Do you think that they might regard it as a philosophical quest, such as would be involved in the 'conquest' of death? Certainly the philosophical approach to questioning the possible outcome of an action is not one that seems to loom very large in the Pardoner's eyes. Is he as drunk in his pursuit of wealth as the rioters are now in pursuing Death and will soon be in their pursuit of gold?

179/188   Blasphemy
177/191   Irony
152/204   Pardoner

181 Whan they han . . .   711/425
The Pardoner allows very little time to elapse in his telling of the *Tale*. In but fifty lines we have met the rioters; learnt of and witnessed their drunken blasphemy which lived down to our worst expectations; seen them warned by both boy and taverner, and ignore those warnings; and witnessed them in drunken rage setting off to find and kill Death after having committed themselves to each other in the strong bonds of brotherhood.

Note the stark contrast of their hasty actions with the quite leisurely preamble of the Pardoner when he dwelt at some length on the nature of those sins and their consequences. It is with almost breathtaking swiftness that his audience is witnessing the fulfilment of all the Pardoner had spoken of.

178/203   Haste
170/238   Rhetoric

182 An oold man . . .   713/427
Note the description of the Old Man, his meekness and poverty, and the gentle way in which he addresses the rioters. The contrast is immediate and startling. Note also that in blessing them he draws only an uncivil answer, a clear comment on the value of all their blasphemous use of God's name – they use God's name, but are unable to respond to it.

168/194   Language
0/184   Old Man

183 The proudeste of thise . . .   716/430
We get very little by way of a description of the rioters. Here, one is distinguished by the name 'proudest', which in this context is not at all complimentary. Can you think why it might be that the persons in the *Tale* have no names – other than in the personification of Death?

174/186   Rioters

184 Why artow al . . .   718/432
The identity of the Old Man is a mystery. Does he and the boy represent the

182/185   Old Man

two extremes of life, youth and old age, neither of whom is successful in turning the rioters from their path?

Is his identity important? Is it more important that he causes their drunken search for Death to be forgotten in their delight in finding gold and wealth, and death? Are we being led to draw analogies with the life the Pardoner leads and make judgements about his fate and the ironies attached to his words? Whether we consider the Old Man as representing Death, the wandering Jew condemned to forever wander the earth, or whoever, what do you consider his function to be?

Given the above questions, should it surprise us that the rioters, drunk as they are, cannot fathom what or who he is?

---

185 And seyde thus . . .   721/435

In direct contrast to the rioters' hasty quest for death, the Old Man has wandered to the ends of the earth 'to Inde', to see if any man would change his youth for 'myn age' – without success. But rather than blindly fight against his plight, he resigns himself to God's will. Note again the contrast between his attitude and that of the three rioters who foolishly set out on an obviously doomed undertaking.

184/186	Old Man

---

186 Ne Deeth, allas . . .   727/441

Can you appreciate the contrast here between the Old Man's desire for death and that of the rioters' quest to kill Death? It is ironic that just as the boy seemed to anticipate the dangers of the rioters' intentions, the Old Man immediately brings up the subject of his own search for death, one that so far has been totally unsuccessful.

175/187	Death
185/187	Old Man
183/189	Rioters

---

187 And on the ground . . .   729/443

The Old Man here picks up the image first introduced by the boy. Is 'modres gate' a reference to Holy Mother Church? Certainly, for the Old Man death does not seem to be something to seek out and kill but rather something to seek out so that it may bring him back to his 'mother'.

168/0	Boy
186/196	Death
173/202	Church
186/188	Old Man

Is his 'mother' life after death, the life that conquers death and which Christ died to achieve for man? Is it being suggested that in seeking to kill Death, the rioters are rejecting the salvation which God provided for them? Certainly their drunken, blaspheming ways would suggest they are rushing headlong away from God.

---

188 Lo, how I vanysshe . . .   732/446

There is an echo here of the blasphemous references detailed by the Pardoner and exemplified by the rioters. Without any blasphemous mention of God's or Christ's bones, flesh or blood, the Old Man gently acquaints them of his desire for death.

180/196	Blasphemy
187/189	Old Man

---

189 But, sires, to yow . . .   739/453

The dignity of the Old Man shows through here as he gently reproves the rioters for their attitude. He uses the same technique as the Pardoner when he supports his reproof with a reference to the Bible but his references are not contrived and blasphemous.

188/190	Old Man
186/190	Rioters

190 Ne dooth unto . . .   745/459
Does this refer to harm in the sense of rough language already used on him, or does he sense the physical harm which these three could so easily vent on him? Is there then a sense of prophecy about the Old Man's words if he is concerned about physical violence?

189/192 Old Man
189/191 Rioters

191 Namoore than that . . .   746/460
Can you see the irony of this comment? He warns them against treating others in a way they would not like to be treated themselves. Yet, shortly after they will plot to do to each other what they most certainly are not expecting to be done to them.

180/192 Irony
190/193 Rioters

192 In age, if that . . .   747/461
Again, the Old Man's comment has a degree of prophetic irony about it – can you see why? Considering this short speech to the three rioters, would you agree that he seems to accurately sense their lack of a future? Is this because he is actually a personification of Death and has 'chosen' his victims well, or is he just an old, wise man who can see from the drunken, blasphemous behaviour of this trio that they are probably not long for this world? Perhaps he is neither and his words are merely fortuitous, or does that deny the craftsmanship of Chaucer in constructing this work?

Think about what else the Old Man might be. Can there be a 'right' answer to this question and can you justify your 'yes' or 'no'?

191/193 Irony
190/197 Old Man

193 And God be with . . .   748/462
Does the Old Man's blessing on them and his apparent desire to end this conversation and be on his way suggest he has seen enough of these men? Why should someone who has spent a lifetime looking for death be in any hurry? What is it that is driving him, calling him, on and away from the rioters? If he is afraid they might kill him it is a strange fear for a man who has unsuccessfully sought death for so long!

192/196 Irony
191/194 Rioters

194 'Nay, olde cherl . . .'   750/464
Note the tone of language and aggressive attitude of this rioter. To what extent does it fulfil the promise of the previous few lines?

182/199 Language
193/195 Rioters

195 Seyde this oother . . .   751/465
Again the author fails to give a rioter the dignity of a name. In doing so, is there a sense in which Chaucer means them to represent the excesses of all men? Is his audience meant to see aspects of themselves reflected in the characters of the rioters?

194/202 Rioters

196 'Thou partest nat . . .'   752/466
We have another reference to 'traytour' Death. Can you conceive of why the rioters consider that Death is a traitor, and to what?

There is a certain irony in this repetition of the term. Presumably Death is a traitor in so far as he kills their friends, though where treachery or falseness comes into such an action is not at all clear. However, look at the sort of treacherous death they will unleash on each other.

188/198 Blasphemy
187/197 Death
193/205 Irony

197 Have heer my trouthe . . .   755/469

What do you consider would make the rioter believe the Old Man was Death's spy? Perhaps he needs no justification at all for such a claim. Certainly the Old Man would seem to have a desire to 'be with' death, but is this sufficient reason for such a claim? Or is it that he is old and dressed in a fashion which raises questions in their minds, as already witnessed when they first met him and commented on his mode of dress?

196/198	Death
192/198	Old Man

198 Telle where he is . . .   756/470

There is a certain pathetic quality about the demand to know where Death is to be found. In one sense, it could be argued that the rioters have already found Death, in that their drunken, blasphemous life has almost certainly led to the 'death' of their immortal souls or perhaps more accurately, death in their rejection of God's grace? Indeed, does the blasphemous reference in the next line contain an inference that the one thing they are missing and which might save them is the 'holy sacrament', Christ's body and blood which they so vehemently and frequently profane in their irreverent utterances?

In his fear of Death, the rioter seems now to have totally convinced himself of the Old Man's identity. Is there a degree of fear also in his implied reference to the Old Man's age when he talks of 'us yonge folk'?

196/0	Blasphemy
197/199	Death
197/199	Old Man

199 'Now sires,' quod . . .   760/474

Despite the roughness of their language towards him, the Old Man still replies in a courteous fashion.

However, in response to their request he immediately tells them where they may find Death. Do you find this strange and does it suggest that perhaps in calling him Death's 'spy' they were being more accurate than they realized?

Does he actually know that Death lies where he says it does, or rather, does he realize the type of men he is dealing with and the likely outcome from what they will discover under the oak tree? Is he simply an excellent reader of character?

198/200	Death
194/210	Language
198/201	Old Man

200 To fynde Deeth . . .   761/475

Note the ironic reference to Death being found along the 'croked wey'.

199/201	Death

201 For in that grove . . .   762/476

Consider why it is that the Old Man who seeks Death should, having found him, then walk away. Perhaps it is that what is under the tree represents no threat to the Old Man, but in his reading of the three rioters' characters, he can see that what is under the oak tree will very easily bring about their deaths. Presuming an absence of threat to the Old Man poses the question: why would it be no threat to him? What does he perhaps lack that they most definitely have – is it avarice? Or should we perhaps look for something more positive in his character than lack of a particular type of sin?

157/204	Avarice
200/202	Death
199/202	Old Man

202 Noght for youre boost . . .   764/478

Is this a warning to the rioters? Is the Old Man placed here to provide the rioters with a last chance to mend their ways?

Is there a significance between the Death to be found under a tree, and the 'tree', the cross on which Christ died? Certainly the Old Man's comment

187/211	Church
201/204	Death
195/203	Rioters
201/0	Old Man

'God save yow, that boghte agayn man kynde' makes a very clear reference to the death of Christ for mankind.

Treated shamefully by the rioters, the Old Man responds with kindness, God's blessing on them and the pious hope that they will amend their ways.

---

203 And evrich of thise . . .   768/482
Note how the counsel and blessings of the Old Man are ignored, bringing to our minds the counsels of the boy and the tavern keeper at the start of the *Tale* which were also ignored. The speed of the narrative is emphasized here as with the Old Man's words still hanging in the air the rioters hasten to their confrontation with Death.

181/206	Haste
202/204	Rioters
169/221	Structure

---

204 Til he cam to . . .   769/483
With the discovery of the money at the foot of the tree, the thought of killing Death flees from their minds almost as quickly as the idea was first conceived.

With this sudden discovery, the desire to meet Death is instantly replaced by avarice, or is it? Would you consider that one of the central themes of the *Prologue* and *Tale* is that the Pardoner's avarice has destroyed the grace in his soul and that through it he has rejected God? Spiritually, the Pardoner is dead. In seeking Death, and finding gold, does the avarice of the rioters lead them to the same fate as that of the Pardoner?

201/226	Avarice
202/228	Death
180/207	Pardoner
203/205	Rioters

---

205 But ech of hem . . .   773/487
From the drunken rage in which they started out we have now swiftly moved to this one peaceful moment when the three rioters sit together, joined in their companionship of greed to contemplate their fortune. Ironically, their companionship does not last long.

196/207	Irony
204/206	Rioters

---

206 The worste of hem . . .   776/490
It is perhaps appropriate that whilst we have no name for him, this particular rioter should be called the 'worste' and perhaps he is. Hardly have they drawn breath after their discovery than we are launched straight into a sequence of events which will assuredly lead to their deaths.

203/218	Haste
205/207	Rioters

---

207 'Bretheren,' quod he . . .   777/491
The reference to 'bretheren' means very little to the 'worste of hem', as little as the drunken determination to kill Death. Would you agree that to date there has been little of substance in their words, in strong contrast to the boy, the taverner and the Old Man?

What use does the Pardoner make of this concept of 'bretheren'? Do you think it would be equally meaningless for him if he were put to the test?

205/213	Irony
204/208	Pardoner
206/208	Rioters

---

208 My wit is greet . . .   778/492
Is there a degree of similarity here between the Pardoner and the rioter? How do they both regard their own intellectual abilities? What evidence would you refer to in support of your views?

207/224	Pardoner
207/209	Rioters

---

209 This tresor hath . . .   779/493
Fortune, or perhaps fate, has delivered riches to them. Fortune will also deprive them of their riches, as we shall see when they decide to murder each other. Their constant blasphemies are a mark of their lack of God's grace. Do you find this is confirmed by their thanks to fortune rather than God?

208/212   Rioters

210 Hoom to myn hous . . .   785/499
Note the sequence of 'myn', 'youres', 'oures'. Why might you sense that in the speaker's mind there is already a doubt as to whom the gold belongs? Whilst he is ostensibly talking about where the gold should be stored, can we assume there is much else on his mind?

He first and rather possessively suggests it should be taken to his house, then realizing that this might be misinterpreted (or perhaps correctly interpreted) by his bretheren, amends the suggestion to 'youres'. However, having mended that one small bridge in the friendship, he hastens to add the qualifying 'this gold is oures'. What can we discover from this as to the effect on him of finding the gold?

204/226   Avarice
199/211   Language

211 Thanne were we . . .   787/501
Note the use of the word 'felicitee' – which means great or true happiness. In the Church's view, such happiness can only be found with God, and in Heaven. May we assume that the Pardoner, in his pursuit of money, thinks to find happiness? Has his avarice and consequent lack of spirituality deprived him of the true treasure, just as the 'felicitee' the rioters have found will prove equally elusive? Indeed, ironically, haven't they already suggested this themselves by the words 'As lightly as it cometh'?

202/215   Church
210/222   Language

212 But trewely, by . . .   788/502
There is effectively a shrewd judgement here on their own characters, when it is suggested they must move the gold by night else be thought of as thieves.

209/214   Rioters

213 And for oure owene . . .   790/504
It is rather ironic that the rioters should fear being hung through a misjudgement of them by others, when they will actually die at the hands of their 'bretheren', and without any attempt at a judgement.

207/224   Irony

214 Wherfore I rede . . .   793/507
The sudden affinity the rioters have developed for 'fortune' is further pursued by the drawing of straws to see which of them will be despatched to town.

212/216   Rioters

215 And brynge us breed . . .   797/511
Is there an implied mockery here of the Holy Sacrament, Communion, in this quest for bread and wine, which though it speaks of Christ's sacrifice and death will here set into train the deaths of the three rioters?

211/236   Church

216 By oon assent . . .   801/515
The place where the gold will be taken has now become even less certain than before – suggesting perhaps the doubts which are besetting the rioters' minds.

214/217   Rioters

217 And it fil on . . .   804/518
The youngest rioter is here despatched to town; is it by trickery? There is no
evidence for this suggestion, but it is reasonable to assume that the other
two might feel he is the least threat and thus the most easily disposed of. In
point of fact, despite his youth he is as corrupt as the others, perhaps even
more so given the plan he devises to kill his 'bretheren'.

216/219   Rioters

218 And forth toward . . .   805/519
The narrative moves with great pace. No sooner have they discovered gold
than the 'bretheren' immediately separate.

206/219   Haste

219 'Thou knowest wel . . .'   808/521
We now have a slight slowing in the pace of the action as the two rioters
carefully sound out each other's attitude to the killing of their 'brother'. The
pace, however, will soon quicken again.

218/226   Haste
217/220   Rioters

220 Thy profit wol . . .   809/524
The obligations imposed by 'sworn brother' are swiftly negated. Note the
conflict in: because you are my 'sworn brother' I am going to suggest we kill
our other 'sworn brother' and steal his share of the gold. Perhaps their
original assumption that they would be assumed to have come by the gold
illegally was not far from the truth.

219/221   Rioters
153/228   Sin

221 Hadde I nat doon . . .   815/529
Note the twisted logic of 'doon a freendes torn to thee', which attempts to
obscure a murderous intent by a 'good' deed. Can you hear echoes here of
the Pardoner's 'many a predicacioun comth ofte tyme of yvel entencioun'?

220/223   Rioters
203/238   Structure

222 That, by my trouthe . . .   823/537
You should by now have had ample opportunity to make judgements about
the value of a rioter's word. Are their words to each other worth anything at
all? Do they mean anything at all?

The same questions could also be asked of the Pardoner.

211/224   Language

223 'Now,' quod the . . .   824/538
The youngest of the rioters has hardly departed before the plan to murder
him is laid bare.

What is the effect of the plan to kill him whilst under the guise of a game?
Do you feel it makes the mockery of their friendship and their pledges as
brothers even more poignant and revolting than it would otherwise have
been?

Why is there the insistence that they should both stab him? It could be to
ensure that the job is done properly, or perhaps there is another reason
which speaks more loudly about the friendship of these two.

221/232   Rioters

224 My deere freend . . .   832/546
Yet again we are drawn by their words to the irony in their use of the terms
friend, brother, companion. You might like to call to mind those duties
which Christ imposed on how we should treat our fellow man and consider
how the three rioters measure up.

213/227   Irony
222/238   Language
208/238   Pardoner

To what extent does their treatment of each other mirror the calculated unconcern for the moral and physical welfare for his fellow man as demonstrated by the Pardoner

---

225 And pleye at dees . . .   834/548
This reference to 'owene wille' brings us back to a central theme of the *Prologue* and *Tale*, that is the wilful rejection of God's grace and goodness and its replacement by the self-centredness of 'cupiditas'.

127/227   Holy Spirit

---

226 This yongeste, which . . .   837/551
Like his friends, the youngest of the three can hardly wait to begin his murderous plotting. His avarice even drives him to make a blasphemous appeal, 'O lord . . .'. Is there almost a reference here to the Pardoner's suggestion that he is about the Lord's work?

210/227   Avarice
219/231   Haste

---

227 Have al this tresor . . .   841/555
Ironically, the rioter has absolutely no intentions of leaving his possession of the gold to fortune as is suggested by 'if so were'. Despite their previous references to fortune, the cupidity of these men is such that fortune plays no part in their affairs. They knowingly choose their paths and know exactly what it is they desire and pursue so avidly. Their rejection of the grace of God, is absolute.

226/230   Avarice
225/230   Holy Spirit
224/237   Irony

---

228 And atte laste . . .   844/558
Whom do you think the 'feend, oure enemy' is – Death, the Devil, avarice, or are they one and the same thing?

204/229   Death
220/235   Sin

---

229 For-why the feend . . .   847/561
In this reference to the life led by the youngest rioter 'in swich lyvynge', and the following comment that the 'feende . . . hadde leve him to sorwe brynge', we see the fulfilment of the warnings given by the boy, the taverner and the Old Man. They were all quite clear about how dangerous an adversary Death was. Perhaps they saw the extent to which the rioters' style of life was a clear invitation for Death to visit them before long.

228/237   Death

---

230 To sleen hem bothe . . .   850/564
Could there be a plainer statement about the condition of this man's soul, a condition brought about by his avarice?

227/234   Avarice
227/239   Holy Spirit

---

231 And forth he . . .   851/565
Again, the terrible sense of urgency which afflicts the rioters is evidenced. However, note how the pace slows down as he pursues the purchase of his poison and wine. Do you find the detail which is given rather strange? Is it necessary? Does it add anything to the content of the sermon which the *Tale* is exemplifying? Consider whether there is any similarity here with the slackening in pace which occurred when the other two rioters discussed the killing of this man.

It is also worth considering the effectiveness of slowing down the pace of the story in this way before allowing it to rush headlong to its inevitable conclusion.

226/235   Haste

232 And preyed hym . . .   853/567
You might consider that rat and polecat were perhaps suitable images for his two friends! Certainly it is impossible to feel any pity for them. It is also certain that by now we could have no feeling for the poisoner either, as he concocts his tale as to why he wants the poison.

223/233   Rioters

233 Than thou wolt . . .   866/580
It would seem that the apothecary is providing him with a fairly slow-acting poison. Is there any reason you can think of why this might be significant, or is it just adding to the sin of this rioter by compounding his murderous intent with cruelty?

232/234   Rioters

234 This cursed man . . .   868/582
Having acquired his poison, in almost feverish haste he rushes around to complete his murderous preparations with always the thought of gold in the front of his mind.

230/243   Avarice
233/235   Rioters

235 What nedeth it . . .   879/593
The descriptions of how the rioters were to go about killing each other were quickly imparted to us. But their actual deaths are even less dwelt upon than the preparations. Perhaps it says something about what the sin of avarice does to a man, to make the preparations for, and the event of, his death worth so little detail and time.

231/0   Haste
234/236   Rioters
228/0   Sin

The warnings they had received since the *Tale* started have been given no regard at all. Do you consider that they deserved all they got, and that, unlike Lot, their drunkenness could not be looked upon as a mitigating circumstance?

There is also the sense here of man being responsible for his own actions, and that the 'fate' he suffers, in so far as his soul is concerned, is one that he knowingly brings upon himself.

236 'Now lat us sitte . . .'   883/597
The depths to which they have sunk are well illustrated here. The determination to sit and drink and make merry are reminiscent of the Pardoner's sermon against drunkenness. To sit and drink against the background of the stabbed and bleeding corpse of their 'friend' dramatically echoes the sins which the Pardoner preached against.

215/242   Church
235/252   Rioters

Is this scene the culmination of so many of the blasphemous references to Christ's body? Would you consider it to be stretching the analogy too far to see in this picture of a dead body, a tree, murderers and the eating of bread and wine, a grotesque image of the Crucifixion? Does the whole story culminate in both the bitter memory and a mockery of Christ's sacrifice on the Cross and victory over death?

237 And with that . . .   885/599
Ironically, the rioters' sudden 'love affair' with fortune takes a turn for the worse, as it 'happed hym, par cas' to drink the poisoned wine.

229/0   Death
227/242   Irony

238 O cursed synne . . .   895/609
Suddenly, the Pardoner launches into the rhetoric which so marked the

224/243   Language

progress of the introduction to the *Tale*. In a few lines he refreshes his audience's mind of the sins his tale has been depicting. Are any of them missed out?

224/239	Pardoner
181/240	Rhetoric
221/240	Structure

239 Allas! mankynde . . .   900/614
The Pardoner's general appeal against the evil-doing of mankind as exemplified in this *Tale* (is this one reason why the rioters are not named, because they personify all men?) again makes a blasphemous reference to 'thy Creatour' to gain substance. Does it need to? Consider the irony of the Pardoner, the very epitome of 'so fals and so unkynde', speaking these words.

230/0	Holy Spirit
238/246	Pardoner

240 Now, goode men . . .   904/618
We now reach the stage, after the telling of the *Tale*, when the Pardoner reiterates for his audience the points he considers most important – but are they important for him or them?

238/241	Rhetoric
238/245	Structure

241 And ware yow fro . . .   905/619
First, we have a reminder about the sin of avarice; the *Tale* just heard of course exemplifies this, but are you aware that it is saying and doing much more?

Note how just after the Pardoner here makes a plea against his audience being avaricious, he immediately demonstrates the same fault in himself.

239/242	Rhetoric

242 Myn hooly pardoun . . .   906/620
Would you consider that perhaps there is an unintentional irony in this statement about 'myn hooly pardoun'?

It could be read as meaning the pardons are personal to the Pardoner, and indeed, given the likelihood of his having forged documents, it could well be so. Equally it might be that he is saying the force of the pardons come from him, personally.

You may recall the proprietary way he referred to 'my pulpet'; is there a sense here that having taken over the pulpit he is now taking over not just some of the Church's functions but also powers that only God could wield, the forgiveness of sin?

236/247	Church
237/254	Irony
241/244	Rhetoric

243 So that ye offre . . .   907/621
Note the linking of the pardon with an immediate reference to payment. The 'so' is conditional: the pardons are only available if 'nobles' or 'sterlynges' are forthcoming. It reflects similar juxtapositions earlier in the *Prologue*.

234/0	Avarice
238/0	Language

244 Boweth youre heed . . .   909/623
Note the clever sandwiching of the request for payment between his promise of 'pardoun' and now this appeal to his credentials in the form of what has been promoted to 'hooly bulle'.

242/249	Rhetoric

245 Cometh up, ye wyves . . .   910/624
The appeal to the wives and for them to 'offreth of your wolle' repeats a very similar appeal earlier in the *Prologue* – do you know where? It also reminds us of his total dedication to acquiring money, even if he has to accept goods in lieu.

240/248	Structure

246 Youre names I . . .   911/625
Do you consider this to be just window-dressing on the Pardoner's part? How good a psychologist do you think he was? Is there a sense here of his offering almost a certain 'pass' into the 'blisse of hevene' if their names are entered in his 'rolle'?

239/247   Pardoner

---

247 I yow assoille . . .   913/627
Even pardoners were subject to some limit to their supposed power! To suggest he can return his audience to the innocent state they were in as new-born babes, upon a simple payment, flouts every teaching of the Church both about pardons and penance.

242/0   Church
246/248   Pardoner

---

248 As ye were born . . .   915/629
The sermon is now finished and the Pardoner speaks directly to his pilgrim audience, as is indicated by a return to the more 'gentil' form of address 'lo, sires'.

247/249   Pardoner
245/0   Structure

---

249 And Jhesu Crist . . .   916/630
Mention was made of this injunction by the Pardoner elsewhere in this guide. You need to attempt some judgement about these lines, but be aware there is no 'correct' answer. As with all such problems, however, some answers are more easily supported than others.

248/250   Pardoner
244/254   Rhetoric

Despite the fact that the Pardoner has obviously finished his sermon, is he so carried away by the effectiveness of his own rhetoric that he cannot stop himself continuing with an attempt to part these pilgrims from their money? Thus, in tune with the openness about his own character that was demonstrated in the *Prologue*, he here continues that 'honesty' with an observation that cannot be quarrelled with. An honesty which is 'guaranteed' by his 'honest' observation 'I wol yow nat deceyve' would seem to suggest that it is a prelude to the reopening of his sales pitch.

Is this a genuine, though perhaps momentary, conversion of the Pardoner by his own rhetoric, a realization of the truth of what he is saying? Does he believe his rhetoric has had the unexpected effect on his fellow pilgrims of making them believe him just as the poor people do? If so, these words are just a mockery of them.

Consider whether the Pardoner is drunk and not really aware of what he is doing, or whether he is perpetrating a joke. He was asked by the Host 'Telle us som myrthe or japes right anon'.

---

250 But, sires, o word . . .   919/633
The presumption of the Pardoner knows no bounds. Do you think the Pardoner really expects the other pilgrims to take his offer seriously?

134/251   Audience
249/251   Pardoner

He refers to having relics from the Pope's own hands. Is this a 'special offer', as it were, to his fellows? Does he expect them to respond positively, or is he being openly ironic and insulting their intelligence? Does he have any respect for any audience? Could the entire performance be regarded as one that he calculated from the start with a view to actually numbering his fellow pilgrims amongst the victims of his – and their – avarice?

---

251 It is an honour . . .   931/645
What do you feel would be the effect on his fellow pilgrims of being told it is

250/0   Audience

	Characters and ideas previous/next comment

an honour for them to have him in their company? Why should he make such a statement? Is this the great actor continuing a performance which is designed to shock?

250/252 Pardoner

In his supreme arrogance is the Pardoner enjoying himself at the others' expense?

252 That I am in . . .   938/652
There is a nice irony here with this reference to 'felaweshipe'. Just as the rioters had no hesitation in plotting to murder and steal from each other, so the Pardoner attempts to lead his audience down the path of avarice with the 'death' of their souls and to steal their money from them with his honeyed words. (You will recall the various connotations of avarice and the sins the Pardoner represents.)

251/253 Pardoner
236/0 Rioter

253 For he is moost . . .   942/656
The Host is not the man to take such an unwarranted insult lying down. It would seem that the Pardoner in the excitement of his rhetoric suddenly overreached himself, and is now to suffer accordingly.

252/254 Pardoner

254 'Nay, nay!' quod he . . .   946/660
If you recall the Pardoner's graphic descriptions accompanying 'At either ende of thee foul is the soun!', do the Host's words carry an echo of them here? Has the 'biter been bit'?

242/0 Irony
253/255 Pardoner
249/0 Rhetoric

255 I wolde I hadde . . .   952/666
As well as expressing the Host's anger, do we also see here an implied comment on the Pardoner's relics? And is there also, for the first time, an open reference to the effeminate appearance and nature of the Pardoner as was so clearly indicated in the introduction to him in the *General Prologue*?

254/256 Pardoner

256 This Pardoner answerde nat . . .   956/670
It is no wonder that the Pardoner should be so angry at this personal attack on him. It is an implied attack on his manhood and one that effectively makes a mockery of the 'man about town' façade that he has been at such pains to present. With the collapse of that façade would all his other pretensions also come tumbling down like a pack of cards: his bulles, his relics, his very pride in his own rhetoric and profession?

255/257 Pardoner

257 Anon they kiste . . .   968/682
Within the context of *The Canterbury Tales* as a whole, we now have to leave the Pardoner and move on to the next *Tale*.

256/0 Pardoner

Give some thought to how you view this ending. In the New Testament the kiss becomes a token of Christian brotherhood. Are we to interpret this particular symbol of brotherhood in the light of the rioters' tale?

Bibliography

There is a huge range of books available on Chaucer, his life, works and times. The following list includes both those which are either easily available and very readable, and also those that, although out of print, are worth tracking down through the public libraries' interlibrary loan scheme.

Chaucer, Derek Brewer (Longmans, 1973, 3rd edition).
 A very readable account of the life and times of Geoffrey Chaucer.
Writers and their Background: Geoffrey Chaucer, ed Derek Brewer (Bell, 1974).
 A selection of interesting essays on a whole range of topics relevant to the student of Chaucer.
Pelican Guide to English Literature, vol 1: The Age of Chaucer, ed Boris Ford (Penguin Books, 1954).
 As well as an essay by John Speirs on the *Pardoner's Prologue* and *Tale*, there is a brief and very relevant section on the social context of Chaucer's times.
The Pardoner's Tale: A Collection of Critical Essays, ed D. R. Faulkner (Prentice Hall, 1973).
 This is out of print, but can be obtained through the interlibrary loan service. This book gathers together many essays on the *Tale* which otherwise would be difficult to obtain and is well worth borrowing.
Set in a Silver Sea, vol 1, Arthur Bryant (Grafton Books, 1985).
 Bryant reviews the history of Britain from 'earliest times to the fifteenth century'. The book provides a fascinating view of the evolution of British society and is written in a most readable style. It makes the history of the times more accessible to the non-specialist student. However, you ought to recognize and be aware that it does project a somewhat rose-tinted vision of the 'special' British character.

Recordings of the *Pardoner's Prologue* and *Tale*

The Canterbury Tales including the *Pardoner's Prologue* and *Tale* and the *Nun's Priest's Tale*, read in Middle English by Robert Ross (Caedmon CDL 51008).
Prologue to *The Canterbury Tales* and the *Pardoner's Tale*, read in Middle English (Argo SAY24 1976, two cassettes).
General Prologue and the *Pardoner's Prologue* and *Tale*. Norman Davis and Neville Coghill, read in Middle English and with a critical discussion (Spoken Arts SAC 919).

Essay writing and examinations

It ought to be obvious to any candidate when the question paper is finally opened and the questions eagerly scanned for those you can answer, that the **question** is what the actual examination paper is all about. The candidate who thinks the examination is about answers looking for questions is sadly misinformed and woefully prepared.

The following notes were written after reviewing examiners' comments on English literature examinations over a five-year period, and covering most of the examining boards in the United Kingdom. They are revealing in the wealth of matter that they have in common.

Answering the question

Discuss . . .
Write an essay on the significance . . .
Consider the portrayal . . . and its significance . . .
Discuss the ways in which . . .
In what senses do you regard . . . ?
Discuss the portrayal . . . with this criticism in mind . . .
Consider the importance . . .
Identify some of the main themes . . . which theme do you consider is treated most effectively?
Do you agree?
To what extent do you consider . . . ?
Can you defend . . . ?
Discuss the role . . .
Consider this comment in relation to . . .
Discuss with reference to . . .

Examinations requiring candidates to answer questions which incorporate such phrases as are illustrated above (taken at random from one board's paper) are actually saying to the candidate, 'We want to know what you think'.

However, it is not as simple as this. They are also saying, 'We want to know what you think about the question we have set you in **this** paper which is lying on the desk in front of you. We want you to read the question carefully, not just part of it but all of it. We then want you to answer that question, not just part of it, but all of it'.

Perhaps this all seems obvious, but the evidence of the examiners' reports suggest that many candidates are failing to gain marks because they have not done what the questions demand of them. Examiners also require that candidates should know **how** to discuss and consider, and that they are aware of the literary implications of what the examiners are asking them to do.

The candidate's first task then is not merely to read the question to be answered, but to study it: to analyse its requirements, hold those requirements at the front of the mind and to prepare the answer accordingly.

Preparation of the answer is essential if you are to ensure balance, development and continuity. As you write your answer, constantly refresh your mind as to the question's requirements. When you have finished your answer, check that it actually answers all the question.

As part of your preparation, take a pen to the question and underline all key words. Jot down on your answer paper all the points the question requires you to answer. As you deal with them, tick them off.

Do not copy out the question or any quoted extract from the text which may be part of the question. It may give you a psychological satisfaction – a false sense of security that you are doing something useful – you are not; an activity such as this is a complete waste of time.

If you go into the examination room and are not thoroughly acquainted with your texts, then no amount of irrelevant detail, quotation, or comment will gain you any marks at all.

Organize your time

Know the requirements of your examination: how many questions you must do and from which sections; the total time allowed; the allocation of marks to questions and sub-sections; and organize your time accordingly. Unanswered questions gain no marks whatsoever. An extra long essay will not magically increase the number of marks allocated to that question by the examiners. Care and balance in your use of the time allowed is essential if you are to do yourself and the examination paper justice.

What are the examiners looking for?

First of all, examiners require an answer to the question. It has already been emphasized but bears repetition.

Whilst you must have a very detailed knowledge of your texts, the examiners are concerned not to test that knowledge, but your ability to make use of it. They are looking for the candidate who has the ability to read a text carefully, closely and thoughtfully and demonstrate a reaction to the text in the examination room. 'The candidate who thinks, and can be seen to think, in the examination room, will always be well rewarded. A sense of mind in action is a central criterion.'

The examiners are not looking for what your teacher, or study guide thinks, but what you think and feel about the text you have studied in relation to the question you are answering. The personal reponse is important, but that does not mean they are looking for you to provide the unique insight into the text which has evaded every critic to date. They do expect you to engage your mind with the text and question and give your considered reaction.

It is not the function of this guide to replace your teacher, and his/her response to your essays will be your best guide as to how they need improving. However, he/she will not be sitting at your elbow in the examination room, so do ensure you take note of what is said in the classroom and the comments made above.

General points to note

1 Learn how to use the possessive apostrophe.

2 Spell the names of characters and authors correctly.

3 Colloquialisms and slang terms, for example 'over the top, gaga, with it, got his act together', merely demonstrate a looseness of thought and expression which is inappropriate for a literature examination.

4 Ensure you have and know how to use an appropriate literary vocabulary. Concepts such as character, drama, narrative, technique, satire, cartoon, farce, comedy, presentation, tragedy, structure, comic, conclusion, diction, tone, symbol, theme,

image, plot, irony etc. should not cause you problems.

Do also note that a mechanical use of these terms without commenting on their effect or function is usually a waste of your time.

5 Where quotation is called for, make it apt and brief. Quotations do not explain themselves. It is up to you, having used them, to point out why and what purpose they serve in relation to your answer. Learn how to incorporate brief quotations into your own prose; if they are too long to be incorporated, ensure that you set them out properly.

6 Do not substitute long pieces of narration or paraphrase for the specific analysis which a question calls for: the examiners will already have a close acquaintance with the text.

If a question does require you to paraphrase do note that it must be in modern English, with the details, tense and person of the original preserved.

Chronology of the age

1300   Mechanical clocks invented shortly before this date.
1303   University of Rome founded.
1305   Units of measurement standardized (e.g. yard, acre) by Edward I.
1313   Invention of the cannon.
1314   The Scots, under Bruce, defeat the English at Bannockburn.
1321   Death of Dante (b. 1265): Italian poet.
1323   Building of Caernarvon Castle completed.
1324   Death of Marco Polo (b. 1254): Venetian traveller and writer.
1327   Reign of Edward III.
1328   Robert Bruce recognized as King of Scotland.
1332?   Origin of Bubonic Plague (Black Death) in India.
1337   Death of Giotto (b. 1267): Florentine artist.
       Beginning of Hundred Year's War between England and France.
1340   Battle of Sluys – English capture the French fleet.
1341   Petrarch crowned as Poet Laureate in Rome.
       Parliament divided into two houses, the Lords and Commons.
1343   Approximate date for birth of Geoffrey Chaucer.
1346   English defeat French at Crécy.
1347   Calais taken by Edward III.
1348   Bubonic Plague reaches England.
1353   Statute of Praemunire: restraints placed on Papal intervention in English affairs.
       Boccaccio's *Decameron* written.
1356   English defeat French at Poitiers.
1360   Edward III makes great territorial gains in France.
       Chaucer taken prisoner at Rheims.
1361   Bubonic Plague strikes England again.
1368   Ming Dynasty in China – lasts until 1644.
       Bubonic Plague recurs.
1369/70   *Book of the Duchess* by Chaucer.
1370   Death of Dafydd ap Gwilym (b. 1340): Welsh poet.
1372/80   *House of Fame* by Chaucer.
1373   Invasion of France by John of Gaunt.
1374   Death of Petrarch (b. 1304): Italian poet.
1375   Death of Boccaccio (b. 1313): Italian author.
1377   Reign of Richard II.
       Poll tax levied.
       Disputed Papal election. Great Schism begins.
1380   Wycliffe's translation of the Bible into English.
1380/86   *Troilus and Criseyde* by Chaucer.
1381   John Ball and Wat Tyler lead the Peasants' Revolt.
1384   Death of John Wycliffe (b. c1324): religious reformer.
1387/1400   Writing of *The Canterbury Tales* by Chaucer.
1390?   Composition of the *Pardoner's Tale*.
1399   Reign of Henry IV.
1400   Death of Geoffrey Chaucer.
       Death of William Langland (b. c1332): poet. Author of *Piers Plowman*.
       Welsh revolt under Glendower begins.
1401   De Haeretico Comburendo: the burning of heretics made legal in England.
1403   Henry IV suppresses uprising under Harry Percy 'Hotspur', at Battle of Shrewsbury.
1413   Reign of Henry V.
1415   English win Battle of Agincourt against the French.

Titles in the series

A level

Coriolanus

GCSE

Animal Farm

The Crucible

Far from the Madding Crowd

Great Expectations

Hobson's Choice

An Inspector Calls

Jane Eyre

Lord of the Flies

Macbeth

A Man for All Seasons

The Mayor of Casterbridge

Of Mice and Men

Pride and Prejudice

Pygmalion

Romeo and Juliet

To Kill A Mockingbird